D1466353

DATE DUE

FERRETS AND FERRETING

FERRETS AND FERRETING

Ian C. Rickard

The Crowood Press

First published in 2003 by
The Crowood Press Ltd
Ramsbury, Marlborough
Wiltshire SN8 2HR

www.crowood.com

British Library Cataloguing-in-Publication Data
A catalogue record for this book is available from the British Library.

ISBN 1 86126 564 6

Dedication
This work is dedicated to the memory of Cally, the best working ferret that
I have had the pleasure of entering to a bury. She was also a most attractive
and good-natured ferret; everyone who met her (save perhaps the rabbits)
fell in love with her and wanted to take her home. Earlier this year, in May
2001 and after a long battle with illness, she passed on. Long will her memory remain.

Line drawings by Marc Rickard.

Typeset by Carreg Limited, Ross-on-Wye, Herefordshire

Printed and bound in Great Britain by Bookcraft, Midsomer Norton

Contents

	Preface	6
	Introduction	7
1	Housing	9
2	Adoption	16
3	Food and Feeding	21
4	Breeding	27
5	Handling	35
6	Introduction to Ferreting	40
7	Equipment	42
8	Obtaining Hunting Rights	57
9	The Art of Ferreting	60
10	Dressing the Kill	72
11	To the Table	76
12	Health and Welfare	82
	Index	96

Preface

My first aim in this book is to dispel some of the long-held myths and falsehoods associated with ferrets. I then hope to help guide the reader through the requirements for housing, and on to selection and acquisition of ferrets. The text will then proceed through food and feeding, breeding and correct handling methods.

The next section relates to working the ferrets. In my view, ferreting is the only truly efficient, humane and organic method of controlling the rabbit population. The reader will be guided through the equipment required, obtaining hunting permission, and on to an introduction into the art of ferreting.

Having caught your rabbits, what will you do with them? The answer is given in the chapter on dressing the kill, followed by some recipes in 'To the Table'. The final chapter deals with the health and welfare of ferrets.

Best wishes for the health and well being of your ferrets, and of those of you who work them. Happy hunting!

Ian C. Rickard

Introduction

The first thing that I am compelled to do is to lay to rest the long held misconception that ferrets are dirty, smelly, vicious creatures. They most definitely are not. Let us take each of these claims or accusations in turn.

Dirty? Never. Ferrets spend a significant portion of their waking hours cleaning themselves. If they are kept communally (which in my opinion, whenever possible, they should be given that they are gregarious creatures), they will extend this action to cleaning and grooming each other.

Smelly? This point has to be approached twice. Hobs (the male of the species) do have a more noticeable aroma during the breeding season. Jills (the female of the species) have very little scent at all. In fact if ferrets are found to have an objectionable odour, the cause of this is most likely to be the fault of an uncaring or lazy keeper, who, through not cleaning the animals' domicile frequently or thoroughly enough, is forcing them to live in unsuitable conditions. The exception to this is that if a ferret is frightened it is capable of giving off a strong odour as a defence mechanism.

Vicious? Not usually. Ferrets can, and sometimes do, bite. On occasions when they do it is usually very painful, but these occurrences are not very frequent and are normally the result of one of three things:

- Defence.
  If any animal feels threatened (humans included), they naturally respond in a defensive manner. The ferret's only real weapons or tools of protection are its teeth; therefore it cannot be blamed for employing them when it perceives the situation to be dangerous.

- Lack of discipline.
  The blame for this lies with us, their human friends. If ferret kits are not handled enough from an early age, and disciplined when they nibble at the handler's fingers, then they do not learn what is and what is not acceptable behaviour. Discipline, in this

instance, must obviously be gentle. Normally all that is required to dissuade the unwanted behaviour is to flick or tap the infant on the nose.

- Incorrect handling.
  The blame for this again lies with humans. If a handler does not hold the ferret correctly, by which I mean that they hold it in such a way that they cause the ferret hurt or discomfort, or hold it too tightly so that it feels threatened, then it will naturally respond unfavourably and could bite. Great care must be taken when handling kits. If, for example, the keeper (or perhaps I should say breeder) attempts to handle kits too soon then the mother may kill and eat her young. The reason for this is not to harm her young as you may think. She is interpreting your intervention as a threat to her offspring, and killing and eating them is her way of protecting them. A further result of this action is that the young are turned into protein, and the Jill will usually return to oestrus very quickly.

All ferrets have different personalities, just like people, and as you get to know your ferrets you will learn how much trust they have in you.

At the time of writing, it is believed that in Europe and the United States of America, ferrets are the third most popular pet behind cats and dogs. Needless to say, ferrets interface with humans in far more ways than just as pets. Whilst they do make excellent pets because they are unbelievably intelligent and friendly, they are often popular entertainment at country shows and game fairs with people exhibiting them in races and fancy ferret shows.

Beyond this, the ferret is also an ally to man when its services are called upon in the working environment as an assistant in the removal of pests. Although this aspect of keeping ferrets is undoubtedly work, it is also a great sport. To the ferret it is just natural behaviour. After all, the ferret is pursuing prey species, as it would have to do to survive in the wild.

Ferrets have been with us in one role or another for thousands of years. Let us hope that they continue to be so for many more.

— 1 —

Housing

Before thinking about selecting the animals themselves, you need first to consider where and how you are going to keep them. Far too often people go out on a whim and acquire a new pet without considering this most vital arrangement. You may be able to get away with it with a cat or a dog, but a ferret is a rather more serious proposition.

KEEPING FERRETS WITHIN YOUR HOME

If you are planning to keep your new friend purely as a pet, you will probably wish to set up its residence within your own home.

There are a number of purpose-built cages and run systems available to buy in pet shops, or you can design and construct your own. Both options have their own advantages and disadvantages.

Commercially supplied facilities are either ready assembled or 'flat pack' for easy self-assembly. The most obvious advantage of these units is the fact that they are very quickly operational and habitable. The greatest disadvantage is that you will probably have to rearrange your home to accommodate the unit. Another drawback is the initial cost, which is likely to be quite high.

The second option is to design and construct your own facility. Provided you are reasonably competent at DIY, this is not as daunting a task as it may first appear, although it will be quite time-consuming. It may also be fairly expensive. The real benefit is that you can custom-build your ferrets' home to blend in with your own home, without having to make too many compromises, thereby getting maximum benefit from the available space.

The framework should be constructed from wood or metal. The levels could be of modular design, to allow the size to be adjusted, and to facilitate easier cleaning. The base unit can accommodate a cupboard for storage of useful ferret-related items such as dry food,

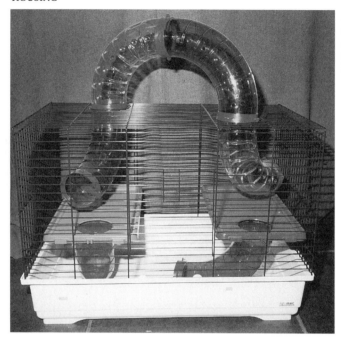

*Example of a
commercially
available
indoor ferret
home.*

food additives, toys, and so on. The bed is in the upper level, the
lavatory position in the bottom level. The outside should be covered
with wire mesh, such as twill weld or weld mesh.

When making a home for your ferrets, it is vital to pay an enormous amount of attention to security. Ferrets are extremely intelligent and adept at the art of escapology. You may be quite happy for
your pet to have the run of your home, but it is far better for it to do
so with your knowledge, rather than without. If your ferret is to be
allowed to run free in the house, you will have to supply litter trays,
preferably one in each room, but at least one on each floor.

You will also have to be aware of the ways in which ferrets can
injure themselves. They may damage themselves on everyday items
left in accessible places, they may be trodden on by visitors or fam-
ily members, or may become trapped in some way, when their own
inquisitive nature leads them astray.

Efficient ventilation must be provided because ferrets, like many
other small animals, have great difficulty in controlling their body
temperature. Over-heating can be seriously detrimental to their
health, and they may even die. On hot summer days, however,

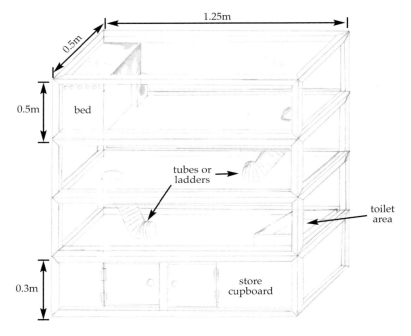

A suitable design for a self-made indoor ferret home.

when house windows and doors are left open, the ferrets will have to be restricted to their cage, or they will very soon escape. Once outside they will be at the mercy of any free-ranging predator, not to mention man and his machines.

KEEPING FERRETS OUTSIDE

Keeping ferrets outside will increase the keeper's workload; feeding and watering operations will be longer, with constant to-ing and fro-ing, as feed dishes are washed and water changed. However, working ferrets should be kept outside. The main reason for this is that work often has to take place in inclement weather. Ferrets that have been kept in a warm house will be nowhere near as hardy as those that have been kept outdoors, and a day's work will take a much greater toll on their body.

When housing ferrets outside you basically have two choices of domicile: cubs or courts.

Examples of outdoor double cage units, built to accommodate one hob in each during the breeding season. The lower ones are two-storey, to give the occupants more room to move around.

Constructing and Siting Cubs

Cubs, or cages, are the smaller of the two options, and should consist of two sections – a bed box and a run. A cub to house two ferrets should be at least 1.5m long, 500cm high and 600cm deep. If you ever have any doubt as to the size always err on the side of caution and build bigger. No animal should be kept in cramped or overcrowded conditions.

The cub should be constructed as sturdily as possible and be waterproof. A rigid frame is constructed from timbers of at least 25 mm square section (I actually use 50 mm square). The top, bottom, back and sides, and the bed door, are made from either marine or exterior plywood at least 9mm thick. All joints in the frame and between the frame and the panels should be bonded together with PVA wood adhesive and either screwed or nailed. The top and sides of the run door are made from timber approximately 30mm wide and 18mm thick. The bottom of the run door should be about 100mm high and 18mm thick. (The extra height of the bottom prevents the egress of the litter used in the run.) The aperture in the door is covered with weld mesh of no more than 13 mm square.

The bed box is about 30cm long and separated from the run by a solid panel with a hole 8–10cm in diameter cut in near the bottom and towards the rear of the cage, to allow the ferrets access to both sections. The bed-box door should be solid, but with vent holes near its top so that the ferrets do not over-heat. Both doors are hinged to allow access for cleaning. Secure locking arrangements should be made so that it is as difficult as possible for anyone to gain access without permission. While guaranteed prevention of theft is virtually impossible, making it as secure as you can will reduce the chance of your animals being stolen.

Once basic construction is completed, the unit should be treated with some form of wood preservative. A water-based product is more likely to be animal-friendly. After the treatment is finished and thoroughly dry the roof of the cage needs to be covered with good-quality mineral roofing felt.

The cage should be situated in a place with as little draught as possible and also as much shade as possible. Direct sunlight should be avoided, because ferrets are particularly vulnerable to heat stroke, a condition often erroneously called 'the sweats' (ferrets are actually incapable of sweating). The cage should also be supported above the ground; this will allow airflow underneath to keep it dry, will stop damp rising up from the ground and causing unpleasant and unhealthy conditions within the cage, and will give better access for cleaning and maintenance routines.

Feed dishes should be removable, as they need to be washed every day. Stainless steel dishes are more expensive, but they are easy to clean, resistant to knocks and bangs, and also less likely to be damaged by the ferrets' teeth. Drinking vessels designed for pet rabbits are inexpensive, manufactured with stainless steel mouthpieces, and readily available at any good pet shop.

Constructing Courts

If you have the space and are considering keeping more than just a couple of ferrets, you may think about constructing courts for them. I have two sizeable courts, one for the jills and one for the hobs in winter. In spring and summer, the hobs are housed separately in cages, because once in breeding condition they do not confine their amorous activities to jills, and this can lead to fighting.

The size of the courts needs only be limited by the space available and financial considerations. To give some idea, mine are each almost 3m long, about 2m high and about 2m wide. They are separated by a small 'walk-in' section, about 1.5m long and deep, and about 2m high. This serves as a useful storage space, but its primary purpose is to act as a containment area for any ferrets that might seek to escape when the court entry door is opened.

The floor of the courts should be concrete, to prevent the ferrets from digging out, and to allow for easy disinfection when necessary.

Mobile bed boxes, approximately 75cm long and 45cm deep and high, provide sleeping accommodation within the courts. They are

The outside walkway in front of my courts.

supported above the concrete floor on 50mm square timbers that are attached to the floor of the box. They are kept mobile so that they can be moved for cleaning; also, in the event of any disease causing problems, the boxes can be easily replaced and the contaminated ones burned.

Four horizontal slots, two at each end, provide ventilation. They are each 12mm high and 50mm long. The roof is removable, secured by two catches, one at each end. Entry and exit is facilitated via a round hole approximately 10cm in diameter, cut in one end of the front face.

The construction method is as used for the cub, except that the timber used is of a much smaller calibre.

Large cat litter trays containing absorbent material provide lavatory facilities, and are easily cleaned. One side is cut out almost to the bottom of the tray, to allow the ferrets easy access. Although cat litter trays are ideal for this purpose, cat litter itself should be avoided. Should the ferrets dig in the litter, as they frequently do, the dust will get into their eyes and other orifices, which is unpleasant and also potentially harmful. Recommended materials include paper, wood chippings, or possibly compacted straw dust.

Drinking requirements are catered for by large versions of pet drinker bottles, fitted into mobile towers. More complex and more efficient provision might be made by the type of nipple system used in some broiler poultry units. The water supply could be direct from the mains, or from a header tank, either manually filled or fed from the mains and controlled by a ball valve. A number of nipples could be installed into each court to deliver water to the ferrets on demand.

The obvious advantage with such a system is that, barring occurrences such as water shortages or mains water failure, the ferrets would never run short of water. Neither would there be any algae growth, which can occur in drinker bottles. On the other hand, a leak might cause the courts to flood, or the system might be prone to freezing in winter – any kind of insulation might be chewed and ingested by the ferrets, causing potentially serious health risks.

Other equipment within the courts might include lengths of pipe, old tyres, branches, balls, piles of stones – indeed, anything that the ferrets can play in or with, without harming themselves. Ferrets are extremely intelligent, and it can be most amusing to sit and observe their antics while they are at play.

The concrete floors of the courts will assist with keeping the ferrets' claws trimmed as they walk on it, but they may be injured if they climb and fall on to it. The floors are therefore covered with a layer of equestrian-grade wood shavings to a depth of 75–100mm. The shavings should be refreshed regularly by raking, topped up when required, and replaced periodically. Equestrian-grade shavings are slightly more expensive, but, being of the dust-extracted type, they are far less likely to cause respiratory problems or discomfort to the ferrets. Ferrets commonly clean their mouths after eating and drinking by rubbing their faces in the litter, and they are also often seen 'ploughing' through them when playing.

It is important to remember that ferrets are natural hoarders; as a result, the shavings or litter must be regularly searched for uneaten remains of food. Should a ferret find stale remnants of food and consume them, this may lead to food poisoning and, possibly, death. There is no excuse in animal husbandry for being uncaring or lazy enough to allow this to happen. There are other considerations too – you will not want the odour of putrefying flesh or stale food, and should wish to avoid attracting flies and the inevitable maggots.

As with the cubs, security is vital and the courts must be locked to deter potential thieves or, for that matter, anyone else who may be harbouring plans for illegal deeds, such as cruelty.

Example of a mobile bed box.

2

Adoption

This chapter title has been chosen with great care. Once you have a home ready and waiting for your new ferret or ferrets, you need to exercise caution in your selection of animals, as this will be a long-term commitment. On average, ferrets have a life span of seven to ten years, but some have been known to live for more than fourteen years. Your future commitment to care for and support your new dependant or dependants will be no less demanding than looking after a child.

There are a number of questions you must ask yourself:

- What is the best source from which to acquire your ferret(s)?
- What age should they be?
- What do you look for to select the right one(s)?
- How many ferret(s) do you plan to keep?
- Which sex?
- What colour?

SOURCES

Anyone planning to acquire an animal is best advised to go to a breeder … but not just any breeder. Some breeders would be better labelled as animal producers and these should be avoided at all costs. Typically, they keep large numbers of animals and continually breed them for as long as they can, purely to make a profit. The animals are rarely properly cared for; they are often kept in substandard or even appalling conditions, they are treated solely as production machines and disposed of when they can no longer fulfil their keepers' requirements.

A good breeder will be proud of his charges. He will be able to tell you the parentage of the kits you are viewing and possibly even their birth date. He will probably watch you carefully when you handle them to decide whether or not he thinks you will be a responsible keeper. His ferrets will be kept in good, clean conditions and will be healthy.

Good breeders need not be difficult to locate. Start by making enquiries at the local veterinary practice. If the vets cannot actually recommend a suitable breeder themselves, they will probably be able to put you in contact with either another ferret keeper or, better still, a local ferret club.

AGE

Generally, the best approach is to purchase a young ferret. Ferret kits should never be separated from their mother any earlier than eight weeks of age, and even this age is too soon, as they still have an awful lot to learn from her. No kit should really be offered for sale at less than twelve weeks old. At sixteen weeks they technically cease to be kits and become ferrets. As a general rule, choose the younger animals, as they will have learnt fewer bad habits and will lend themselves to being trained more easily.

SIGNS OF A GOOD FERRET

Watch your prospective purchases in their cage or run. A good healthy kit or young ferret will be bouncing about, full of life and playing with its siblings. It will have a good shine to its coat and be 'bright-eyed and bushy-tailed'. Any that lie around lethargically or seem to lack any interest should be avoided.

Handle them all. If any seem to lunge at fingers or hands, trying to bite or nip, more than the rest, consider them with caution.

Examine all the animals. If any show signs of discharge from anatomical orifices, or display any other signs of illness, discount them from your deliberations. You may also prefer to discount all those from the same cage as the sick animal; they may not yet be displaying any signs of illness, but they will probably be infected, and would then be liable to spread the disease to any other ferrets that you may have.

If possible, see the parents and handle them too. If they display vicious, aggressive tendencies, consider their kits with caution. They will almost certainly pass on those traits to their progeny. Although, with care, it should be possible to train those aspects of their character out of them, it is much easier not to have to contend with them in the first place.

NUMBERS AND SEX

The question of how many animals to have is one that you will have to answer prior to obtaining or designing your housing arrangements. Ferrets are gregarious creatures and will be far happier with other members of their species to keep them company than on their own.

If you are planning to keep more than one ferret, then the question of gender has to be approached. If you have no plans for breeding, clearly it is not a good idea to keep opposite sexes together. Also, a hob kept with an in-season jill will potentially mate and re-mate with her to the exclusion of other activities, possibly leading to his death, and her injury.

Jills (females) will come into season in the spring, regardless of whether or not hobs are present. They must be taken out of season for health reasons. If they are allowed to stay in season for prolonged periods of time, they will become very ill and will probably die. There are two common illnesses. Pyometra is the accumulation of pus within the animal's uterus, and is more common after the start of a pseudo or phantom pregnancy. Left untreated, the animal will almost certainly die. The second condition, oestrogen-induced anaemia, can have seriously detrimental effects on the animal's health, and can sometimes lead to a progressive depression of the bone marrow. This may result in another condition, called pancytopoenia, the abnormal depression of all three elements of her blood; it is debilitating and potentially fatal.

These two ferrets are actually litter siblings (hob left, jill right). This illustrates the difference in size relative to gender, or, more correctly, the 'sexual dimorphism'.

These conditions can be avoided in a number of ways. Assuming that you do not want to breed from the jill, you can have her served (mated) by a hoblet (vasectomized male ferret), to induce a phantom or pseudo pregnancy. Alternatively, a vet can give her a 'jill jab' (an injection of hormones to take her out of season). Both of these methods will have to be repeated each time she comes into oestrus. A third option, assuming that you know that you will *never* want to breed from her, is to have her neutered or spayed by a vet.

Kept together, multiple complete hobs or hoblets, or any combination thereof, may fight. If you particularly wish to keep male ferrets together, you may have them castrated (this action results in them now being called 'hobbles'). They will no longer have the desire to mate and will normally live peacefully together.

Once the above considerations have been taken on board and decisions relating to them made, there are really only two other questions to be answered: how much space do you have available (over-crowding is not acceptable), and how many ferrets can you afford to feed?

The choice of sex could also depend on whether you are planning keeping ferrets as pets or for working purposes. Both sexes can make excellent pets or working ferrets, however both do have their own inherent problems.

If you intend to keep them as working animals, the type of work that you have in mind has to be considered. Generally speaking, hobs tend to be approximately two to three times the size of jills. As with all animals, there is no guaranteed size, but this sex difference can present you with problems. For example, if you intend to use them only for ratting, hobs may find it difficult to get into many holes, and jills would be best. There are fewer problems with rabbiting, although hobs do occasionally find it difficult to enter rabbit burrows. Another consideration is that a large ferret will probably find it more difficult to manoeuvre in smaller tunnels.

Some claim that hob ferrets work faster than jills, but this is not my experience. Indeed, one of my fastest and best ferrets was a jill called Cally (who is remembered in the dedication at the front of this book).

As pets, there is no reason for either sex to be considered better than the other, although multiple hobs will need to be housed separately in the breeding season, in order to prevent fighting.

The only other point to consider is health. Jills must be continually taken out of oestrus during the breeding season to prevent them from developing serious, potentially life-threatening health concerns (*see* page 92).

COLOUR

For ferrets kept only as pets, the question of colour is purely a matter of personal preference, but for working ferrets there may be operational considerations. Clearly, if you are paying proper attention to the job in hand it should make no difference what colour your ferrets are, but any advantage that can be gained is more than welcome. If you are working on frost- or snow-covered ground, it is far easier to see a dark ferret exiting the burrow. On the other hand, if you are ferreting under a hedge or bramble, it will be much easier to see a light ferret.

The opposite ends of the colour scale: an albino (above) and a poley (below).

3

Food and Feeding

NATURAL DIET

Ferrets are carnivores, or meat eaters. In the wild, their natural diet would be one of meat, which would be hunted down, killed and eaten. Their taste is broad and varied, including any form of flesh, whether from mammals, birds, fish, reptiles, worms, or even slugs and snails. They catch and kill their prey, then proceed to eat it – the whole carcass. Just because they are living in captivity, why should their diet be different? How on earth can anyone justify keeping an animal, whose natural diet is as above, on milk sops (a mixture of bread and milk)? It is no wonder that in the past captive ferrets led very short lives in comparison with the expected norm.

Logically, the best diet would be as above, although it is recommended first to remove the stomach and intestines (the thin skin and rubbish will probably end up as a mess in the court or cage). The liver should be inspected for signs of disease and discarded if any is found. The fur or feathers should be left on as this provides fibre in the diet, but beware of the fact that you may be introducing ticks or fleas. Pouring boiling water over the cadaver may prevent this.

Under no circumstances should the carcass be left in the ferrets' domicile until it is all gone; remove whatever is left the day after its introduction. Remember that ferrets are natural hoarders so you must search carefully for any remnants and remove them *all*.

ALTERNATIVES

The ferrets must be fed daily. Unfortunately, unless you are very lucky, it is highly unlikely that you will acquire enough cadavers to feed your ferrets continually on their natural diet. Therefore another source of food will have to be found and used.

Cat and Dog Food

There are a number of commercially produced canned cat and dog foods on the market, not specially formulated for ferrets, but an acceptable alternative. Generally speaking, cat food tends to have a higher protein value and is therefore the better of the two options. You may also like to add a vitamin supplement such as Intervet SA-37, available in 200g tubs and 2kg tubs. It is usually available from good pet shops or veterinary surgeries. Alternatively, ask your vet for a recommendation.

Day-Old Chicks

Day-old chicks are believed to be a good source of food, which is relatively inexpensive and fairly freely available. However, its frequent use is not recommended. Research has shown that the food is low in some essential requirements, leading to serious health problems such as osteodystrophy, hypocalcaemia and thiamine deficiency, among others. Another complaint caused by excessive feeding of

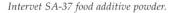

Intervet SA-37 food additive powder.

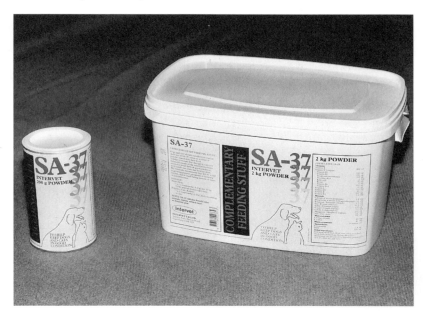

day-old chicks is actinomycosis, which causes the throat to thicken and swell. It is thought to be the result of abrasions within the oesophagus. Ferrets may be given chicks occasionally, but not more than once or twice per month.

Dry Foods

Much research has been carried out in the field of animal feeds and you can now go into any good pet shop and buy specially formulated dry food for ferrets. While this is not 'natural' food for them, it is specifically designed and formulated with ferrets in mind. Their faeces will be firmer, and smell less strongly. Another advantage is that, as long as it remains dry, the food will not go off and can therefore be left in the ferrets' domicile continually so that they may feed at will. If you decide to feed your ferrets in this way, you will have to supply them with copious amounts of water to prevent dehydration.

It is always a good idea to keep some dry food available in case of emergencies.

FEEDING MY FERRETS

I am fortunate enough to have access to a good regular supply of chicken trimmings from a commercial food outlet. I also collect supplies of lights (animal lungs) and tracheas from a butcher from whom I also buy some liver and ox hearts. When available, damaged rabbits and rabbit offal are also included. These raw supplies are cut into more manageable strips and cooked. After cooking, the liquid is drained off and the meat left to cool. When it is cold, it is minced and mixed thoroughly. It is then bagged and frozen into quantities that are sufficient to feed my ferrets for about a day or so. Obviously it has to be defrosted thoroughly prior to feeding. When it is fed to the ferrets it is distributed into their dishes, with a suitable measure of Intervet SA-37 sprinkled over it.

This process is time-consuming, but there are some good reasons for it. Cooking is done for two reasons. First, the food does not go off as quickly as it would if it were left raw, and it does not seem to attract as many flies. Second, a ferret that is used to the taste of raw meat and blood is more likely to eat and lie up when working; feeding cooked food seems to reduce this problem. I have dug out ferrets that have both killed and mauled or savaged rabbits, but I have never had to dig out a ferret that has killed and eaten.

Mincing is a good idea for two reasons. First, if the food is left in larger pieces the ferrets may well squabble over who has what; when it is minced, they cannot do this. Second, if it is left in large chunks, the ferrets can carry it off and hoard it. Mincing therefore reduces the risks of stale food being hidden in the courts or cages and the consequent risk to the ferrets' health.

My ferrets are generally fed on the above and, occasionally, on dry food. Their general health and condition is good and they have all lived long and happy lives.

FOOD ADDITIVES

The food additive Intervet SA-37 is purchased in powder form. When the ferrets are not being fed specially formulated ferret food or cadavers, a measure of this compound is sprinkled over the food prior to feeding. It is a balanced mix of essential minerals and vitamins that is specially formulated to enhance animal feedstuffs. At the time of writing, it is undergoing a reformulation to improve it still further by its manufacturers.

An arrangement of ferret health and hygiene products, available from Shaws Pet Products.

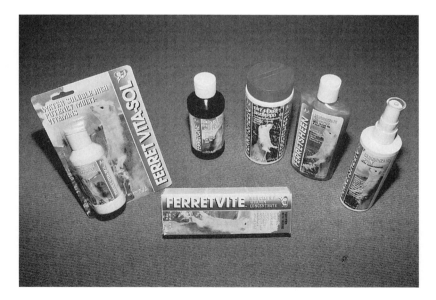

Another supplement that is particularly useful if a ferret seems to be off its food is Ferretvite, a high-calorie vitamin concentrate that comes in a 120g tube. It is produced by Shaws Pet Products Ltd (telephone 01296 429333, email info@shawspet.co.uk).

Other products available from this company include water additives, shampoos and treats.

DRINKING

Ferrets should always have a good supply of clean, fresh water, preferably delivered to them via small animal drinking bottles (*see* page 14). If you are keeping large numbers of ferrets together or feeding on dry food, you will need to use either multiple small drinking bottles or larger bottles to cope with the demand. These bottles are hygienic and easily cleaned. The spouts are also manufactured from stainless steel so they are able to resist the ferrets' teeth.

If drinker bottles of this type are used, the *inside* of the spouts must be inspected frequently and thoroughly to check for any build-up of limescale deposits, particularly if you live in a hard-water area. If found, they must be removed. Failure to carry out this simple task can lead to blocking of the spout, which will severely restrict the ferrets' water intake.

A stainless steel food dish, as recommended, suitable for feeding one ferret.

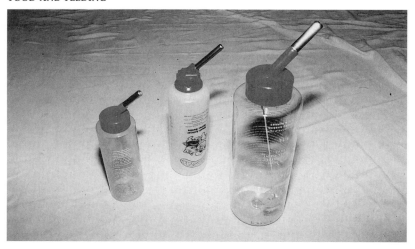

A selection of drinker bottles. The white plastic one in the centre is by far the most resilient, and marginally more expensive.

Alternative options to this method are dishes or mains water supplied through drinker nipples, as used in the broiler poultry industry.

Drinker dishes or bowls are not recommended, as the ferrets can walk through them and they are also open to the elements, with all types of matter getting in and polluting the contents. They are also easily knocked over and spilled. This is not only messy, but also leaves the ferrets short of water, leading to possible dehydration. Ferrets kept in damp, unhygienic conditions are also at risk of health problems such as foot rot. In addition to this, if you are considering breeding, you have the added hazard of kits getting in and drowning.

The drinker nipple option may be very efficient in the poultry industry, but it is not ideally suited to this environment. When used in the poultry industry it is installed into heated sheds, while ferret cages are generally more exposed. This fact alone predicts serious complications with freezing. It would be difficult to insulate the system because of the likelihood of ferrets chewing and tearing the lagging material. The nipples themselves could not be insulated, as this would prevent them from working. Whilst it may be a viable proposition to introduce this method if your ferrets are housed in courts, it is almost certainly not logistically viable if your housing takes the form of multiple cages.

4

Breeding

REASONS FOR BREEDING

Breeding is not to be taken lightly, and novice ferret keepers are not advised to attempt it. Before embarking on a breeding programme, you should have reasonable experience in the field of ferret husbandry, and you should examine your reasons for wishing to breed very carefully. If you think that at the end of your breeding season you are going to have made a small fortune, save your time and effort. Young, developing ferrets have a voracious appetite and will eat enormous amounts of food. Therefore, considering the relatively small price that ferrets fetch at point of sale, the cost of rearing is prohibitive.

There are a number of justifiable reasons for embarking on a breeding programme. Should you wish to replace missing or old ferrets from your own string, why not try breeding your own? Similarly, if you are trying to improve on the working abilities of your current stock, it is worth looking into it. However, it is vital to remember that, although a jill only has eight nipples, she can deliver and, if fed correctly, raise more than eight kits. Ferret litters vary in size between one and fifteen, although the average is probably about six to eight. If you are looking to expand on your current string, you will probably only want to keep one or two for yourself. This means that you will almost certainly be left with a surplus. If possible, you should always have 'tested the water' to try to find suitable homes for them. Do not assume that, once you have got what you want, you can just dump the rest on to a ferret rescue. There are far too many homeless ferrets out in the world already.

RECORDS

One of the most essential requirements in any breeding programme is good, efficient and careful record-keeping. Records can be kept in any number of ways – loose-leaf pads, card indexes, notebooks or even on a personal computer. Database software such as Microsoft Access is particularly useful, and records can be printed off in report form for use in loose-leaf pads. The system you choose should be as user-friendly as possible while remaining comprehensive.

Each and every ferret should have certain details recorded about it: name, colour, date of birth, parents, maternal and paternal grand-parents and great-grandparents. It may also be useful to record the number of kits born in its litter and how many survived.

THE BREEDING SEASON

Ferrets are photoperiodic. This means that the animal's brain decides when the breeding season starts and finishes according to the amount of light available. In nature, as the daylight hours increase in the spring, the animals come into season or breeding condition. Conversely, as the number of daylight hours decreases, as winter approaches, they go out of season. This means that if he so desires a keeper can control when his ferrets come into and go out of season by the use of artificial lighting. However, this is generally the prac-tice of the aforementioned animal producers, for their own gains

It is easy to see when a jill comes into season, or a hob into breed-ing fettle. If left to nature, as spring approaches the jill will come into oestrus. On examination you will see that the jill's vulva (her vaginal orifice, just below her anus) will swell and protrude from her body by around a centimetre. There may well be a visible dis-charge and she will probably smell more strongly. She may well become bad-tempered and irritable owing to the hormonal imbal-ance. If she is not mated or given a jill jab by a vet she will remain in season until the end of the summer, if she lives that long. This should not be allowed to happen because of the serious detrimental effects that it would have on her health (*see* page 92). If you wish her to produce a litter she should be placed with a hob that is in fettle. If you do not wish to breed from her, she should either be placed with a hoblet (a vasectomized hob), or given a jill jab.

With hobs, and hoblets, as spring approaches their testicles enlarge and descend from within the abdominal cavity into the scro-tum. Whilst they are capable of performing the physical act of mat-

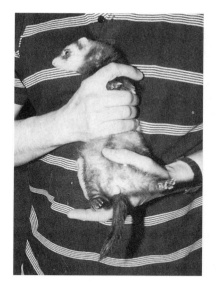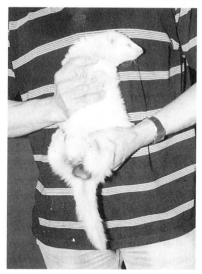

A jill in season (left) and a hob in breeding fettle (right).

ing before their testicles have descended, hobs will be infertile. Hoblets are infertile whether their testicles have descended or not. If you wish to breed, you must wait until a hob's testicles have fully descended. This should not pose a problem because in my experience hobs tend to come into breeding fettle before jills. At the end of the breeding season, as winter approaches, hobs and hoblets also come out of fettle. Their testicles shrink and are retracted back into the abdomen.

MATING

Having selected the pair from which you wish to breed, you must wait until the jill is fully in season. This is when the vulva is fully extended or swollen, and is usually about ten to fourteen days after swelling begins. Remove the jill from her cage or court and introduce her to the hob in his cage. It is safer to present them to each other in this manner because the jill is then entering the hob's territory and is more likely to be submissive. If any food is present in the cage, remove it to make sure that it is not a possible bone of contention between them (although this is highly unlikely).

29

Shortly after the introduction, usually within the first minute or so, the hob will have taken the jill by the neck, dragged her to a place of his choosing, and penetrated her. This ordinarily occurs in the bed box, but not always. They will remain coupled for some time, possibly hours. Following this the hob will drag the jill around the cage by her neck, and her head may be seen or heard to impact on the structure of the cage. The hob will probably mount her repeatedly. You may be tempted to intervene and separate them to protect the jill, but you should not. The actual mating process is very violent, and it is necessary for it to be so in order to induce ovulation. Ovulation typically occurs thirty to forty hours after copulation.

After mating the two ferrets will probably clean themselves, have a drink, and in all likeliness go to sleep. If they are left together the hob, when ready, will repeat the whole process. After several hours the pair should be separated, and the jill examined for signs of dam-

A typical example of the mating process. The hob, behind, has grasped the jill by the scruff of her neck.

age, particularly around her neck. If any is found it should be bathed gently with a strong solution of saltwater to prevent infection. Any wounds that are leaking or exuding fluid should be dusted with antiseptic wound powder. Assuming that the pair were together for around twenty-four hours, she should be pregnant. However, if you want to be sure, you can place them together again after a couple of days and the process will be repeated. You should always allow them to rest for at least a day between mating sessions.

Within ten days of the coupling, the swelling of the vulva should begin to diminish, and it should have returned to normal size in approximately two to three weeks.

The gestation period (term of pregnancy) in ferrets is forty-two days, however one or two days either side is not unusual. The jill can be returned to her court with the other jills for the first month. She should then be removed and settled into a cage on her own for the last ten to fourteen days so that she can build a nest and prepare for the birth. When reviewing her condition do not be overly concerned if she should shed her guard hairs (the longer, coarser hairs) during the latter stages of her pregnancy and be reduced to her short soft undercoat. This is not unusual and often quite normal. She should not be picked up or handled at all during the last three or four days of her pregnancy. Any handling during her pregnancy must be done with great care, and particular attention must be given to supporting her body weight from the rear end to minimise the risk of spinal injury arising from her increased body mass and the additional weight being suspended on it.

Palatable food and water should be available twenty-four hours a day. If she is carrying a large litter, the intra-abdominal space available for food will be reduced so she will eat little and often. She will typically drink three times the volume of water pro rata to the volume of dry food, and if she is allowed to run out of water at any point she will stop eating. Particularly during the latter part of her gestation period it is recommended that she be given a high-calorie nutritional supplement.

BIRTH AND REARING

At birth, kits are blind, deaf and naked, and totally dependent on their mother. They suckle milk from her for the first four to six weeks, despite the fact that they are capable of eating solids from about three weeks of age, and often do. In fact, if a jill has a large litter, it is advisable to take small dishes of warm milk and sometimes egg yolk and milk to her, to help keep her well nourished and assist her with her task of rearing. In the interests of safety and hygiene, you should remain with her, holding the dish, until she has had all she wants, to ensure that it does not get spilt.

It is important not to disturb the nest in any way for at least a few days. When visiting the nest in the early stages, rub your hands in the litter of her run and then let her smell them prior to approaching the nest. If she is a mature jill and you know each other well you should not have any problems, but it is not worth taking a risk. If she feels that her litter is threatened in any way she will kill and eat them. This action is quite normal to her. (It is her way of protecting them.) The kits are converted back into protein, and the jill is brought back into season ready to continue procreation.

Providing you give her a suitable diet, rich in proteins, fats and carbohydrates, the jill will not normally have any problems raising even very large litters. Despite the fact that she has only eight nipples, she is able to raise more than eight kits.

When she is nursing, close attention must be paid to her condition. It is not unusual for her to lose some weight, but if she should lose a lot of weight, or her condition should deteriorate significant-

A litter of kittens, one day old.

ly, her diet should be considered and professional veterinary advice sought. Another condition to be guarded against is mastitis, the inflammation of the mammary glands or nipples. Ferrets are extremely hardy creatures, and they very often do not exhibit obvious signs of ill health until it is too late to help them. Having said that, if you care for your ferrets properly and examine them regu-

A litter of kittens, approximately nine days old.

larly (every day is not unreasonable), you should notice the onset of any problems.

The birth weight of kits is normally 8–10g. Kits grow rapidly and will probably double in size within the first twenty-four to thirty-six hours. In dark-coloured kits the fur may start to be visible within the first week. They will normally have a good covering by the time they are four weeks old.

Deciduous teeth break through at between ten days and a fortnight of age, but the canine teeth appear significantly later – at around seven to eight weeks old – along with their permanent teeth. In some instances, kits of two to three weeks of age will manage to crawl out of the nest, only to be dragged back in by the mother. This is no mean accomplishment on their part, given the fact that they are still blind and deaf; their ears and eyes do not open until they are between three and five weeks old. Be warned though, as this may be indicative of the fact that the mother is unable to nourish them all adequately, and they are going in search of food for themselves.

Weaning will occur at around eight weeks of age, although the kits should not be bought or sold until they are at least twelve weeks old. Kits should not be separated from their mother until they are twelve weeks of age as they are still learning from her.

A jill with her litter, approximately three weeks old.

5

Handling

HANDLING KITS

First Steps

Handling your ferrets is something that must begin as soon as possible. If you have bred them yourself, and the jill knows and trusts you, you may be able to handle the kits from a very early age. Otherwise, you should wait until the kits start to leave the nest and move around the cage, which will probably be at about three weeks. First, prepare your hands by rubbing them in the litter of the run, then let the mother smell them and handle her gently. In some cases it may be necessary to remove her and confine her in a box if she is over-protective. After doing this, you should be able to handle the kits. Stroke them gently. Pick them up very carefully and support their body completely. Always handle them individually. If they try to nip or nibble at your fingers tap them gently on the nose – remember that they are very young and fragile. (Although the nips and nibbles can be uncomfortable, they could not be described as particularly painful.)

Next Stages

Once the first step has been overcome, the kits will become more and more used to you with regular handling. The next stage is to take a container of warm milk with an egg yolk mixed in it. Place the container somewhere safe where it will not fall or be dislodged. Again, pick the mother up first to reassure her that you mean no harm, then settle her back in the cage, or in the box if necessary. Pick up the kits one at a time and hold them gently but securely in one hand. Dip the fingers of your free hand into the milk mixture and encourage the kit to lick it from your skin. Again, if they nip or nibble, tap them gently on the nose. Always finish with each kit with it feeding successfully from you, not being disciplined, and then return it to the cage or nest.

The next stage, logically, is for the kits to graduate on to solid food, taken from your fingers or picked up from your hand. Small quantities of scrambled egg or crumbled yolk of hard-boiled egg serve well, along with small morsels of their usual food. If you are feeding dry food you will need to soften it first by soaking it in water.

Correct methods of holding ferrets: thumb and forefinger around neck, arms between first and second fingers (below), or, alternatively, by the scruff of the neck (opposite). In both cases, the ferret's body weight is supported by the other hand.

If you follow this routine carefully you should not experience any problems with handling your ferrets.

HANDLING ADULTS

The methods used for picking up and handling an adult ferret are different from those used for handling a kit because the adult is significantly bigger. Ideally, holding your hand open, palm upwards, in front of the animal, and encouraging it to walk on to it with a command such as 'lift' is by far the best way. When it has passed

The alternative method of holding a ferret: see opposite.

over your fingers and has its hands on the palm of your hand, gently curl your index and middle fingers upwards – one on each side of its chest, behind its shoulders – and carefully lift it. Place your other hand under its hindquarters as soon as possible to give support to its body weight.

If the ferret does not lend itself to this manner of picking up, position your hand so that the thumb and index finger are around its neck and the other three fingers are around and under its chest. Again, as soon as possible, support its hindquarters with your other hand. Never hold the ferret tightly around its neck. This type of grip is known as 'strangling' and will very soon result in the ferret becoming defensive, probably struggling and biting to get free. If a ferret should wriggle or struggle, the natural reaction is to tighten your grip. Resist it, as this sets in motion a vicious circle of struggling and gripping more tightly – with disastrous consequences. Either the ferret may be injured, or you bitten, or possibly both.

Another option is to pick the ferret up like a cat, holding it by the scruff of the neck. This method has certain advantages – for example, it is useful if the ferret is prone to biting, it can make ferrets more docile and quiet, and it makes it much easier to open the mouth to examine teeth and dental hygiene – but its regular use is rather brutal.

When going to pick up a ferret, do not lunge quickly at the animal, particularly from above. This kind of action will cause the ferret to view you as a predator, and to react defensively, probably biting first and finding out what it has bitten later. It will also result in the ferret becoming nervous and consequently difficult to pick up. Your ferrets are your friends, and as such they should have no reason to fear you. If your ferrets are pets this problem is bad enough, but if you work them it will probably result in them becoming 'skulky'. Skulky ferrets have a tendency to back away down the rabbit hole instead of coming forward to you. Obviously this makes it difficult to recover them when you have finished at a particular bury, resulting in lost time and sometimes lost patience. Both situations can easily mar an otherwise enjoyable day's sport.

BITERS

If you take on an adult ferret with a tendency towards biting, it is not impossible to re-train it in a similar way to training kits. The training will, however, be far more time-consuming and potentially more painful. You will have to break the bad habit before you can introduce a good one.

Hold the ferret in one hand, and offer it the chance to bite the knuckles of the other hand. Make sure the 'sacrificial' hand is in a clenched fist and the ferret can only get to the knuckles, not loose flesh. As much as possible, when the animal attempts to bite, withdraw the hand and flick the ferret firmly on the nose. Continue this until the ferret starts to lose some of its aggression. This process may well take several days. When it has started to calm a little, offer it a treat on the outstretched palm of the hand; you may also find it useful to spit in your hand, as ferrets generally love human saliva. This works twofold – the ferret gets a drink and also learns to appreciate the smell of you.

About six years ago, I acquired a kit of approximately six months of age. A persistent biter, he did not respond at all to the 'carrot and cane' treatment described above. As a last resort I decided to try something a bit different. I rubbed some neat, undiluted disinfectant into my hands. (Always be extremely careful when using disinfectant in or around ferrets and their homes. Some disinfectants contain Phenol, which will burn the ferret's skin. It is easily identifiable because it turns water milky.) I went back to the ferret's cage and offered him my hand. He attacked as if to bite, but when his tongue touched my skin he pulled away, shook his head and spluttered. He made a few more attempts that day, with the same results. I continued this course of action for about four or five days and he lost all interest in biting. He has now become one of the softest, most lovable ferrets I have.

In the past it was considered perfectly acceptable to break off a ferret's teeth with pliers, so that they could not do as much harm if they tried to bite. This type of behaviour was nothing short of barbaric. Similarly horrific was the practice of preventing biting and killing underground by stitching a ferret's lips together.

Slightly more humane was the practice of muzzling, still used by some today. If you ever decide to resort to this method, you should never use anything other than thin cotton. Should you lose the ferret, the cotton will soon rot and the ferret will then be able to feed itself. With the tracking devices available today you should not lose a ferret, but you must allow for the eventuality.

The above methods of restraint should be totally unnecessary and they range from the unkind to the barbaric, not least because the ferret will be unable to defend itself against another predator such as a rat, stoat or weasel. The simplest and kindest answer is for the keeper to take proper care of his charges and when necessary train them not to bite.

— 6 —

Introduction to Ferreting

Now onto the second part of this book's title and one of my favourite interests. Ferreting. As a sport, I personally consider it to be unrivalled.

Imagine: it is a nice crisp morning and you gather your equipment together, box up your ferrets, and meet up with some friends. You travel out to your chosen site for the day, alight from your vehicles, and fit the ferrets with their locator collars (assuming that this has not been done prior to leaving home). You divide up the equipment and set off in search of coney.

You travel as quietly as possible so as not to forewarn your prey of your presence. A simple oversight such as stepping on and breaking a branch for example will be a grand announcement to any wildlife of the potential danger that you pose to them. You use all of your fieldcraft and experience, walking silently, reading the terrain for evidence of rabbit damage, looking for signs such as droppings or fur, sniffing the air for the unmistakable scent of an active rabbit bury. You are all eagerly awaiting the first net strike of the day.

Here it is, an apparently busy bury. You scout it carefully, walking softly. It is not very big – only an eighteen-holer. You set to work quickly and quietly, clearing the debris that could so easily foul a net, and net it up. Two ferrets are selected. You ensure that their locator collars are working correctly by switching on the receiver near to them and comparing the readings on the dial with the estimated distance between the units. Any other ferrets or active collars are removed from the immediate vicinity to prevent confusing signals being recorded. The chosen pair are entered at opposite ends of the bury. Now, stand back out of sight of the holes and wait.

Someone indicates silently that a ferret has surfaced. She is carefully encouraged to return to her task, or alternatively lifted and re-entered into a different hole that has not yet been visited by either of them. All is still once more. Then, suddenly you hear a rumble, the ground beneath your feet vibrates. The game's afoot. Smiles of anticipation spread through your company. Each person watches

A team of two: my brother and I ferreting a hedgerow bury.

their allotted holes, and tries to help watch each other's, senses tingling with anticipation. There's another rumble, and another, then ... *whoosh*! A rabbit hits a net; it purses beautifully. You pounce on it instinctively, placing your foot over the hole to prevent a double bolt. Another member of your party attends the scene with a spare net to re-net the hole. Their presence frees you up to remove the rabbit from the net and despatch it quickly and painlessly with a flick of your wrist, breaking its neck. A great start to what you hope will be a great day on the land.

— 7 —

Equipment

The equipment required to begin ferreting is not particularly expensive. As you gain experience, you will gradually acquire more bits and pieces to make various tasks easier, but to start off with there are just a few absolute basics:

- appropriate clothing;
- purse nets;
- spade;
- knife;
- ferret-carrying box;
- ferrets.

A collection of basic equipment.

Dry-weather outer garments (right), and wet-weather outer coverings (below).

CLOTHING

Too many people make the mistake of embarking on their first ferreting trip without considering this vital issue. Much of the time you will be going out in inclement weather, and you will need to wear warm, waterproof clothes. You can keep warm easily by wearing multiple layers of old clothes, and putting on waterproofs over the top when required. However, you must give some thought to the outer layers.

If a rabbit comes to the mouth of the hole and looks out prior to bolting, as they sometimes do, and sees a brightly coloured anorak, he is not likely to bolt (unless the ferret is right behind him). If he turns and goes back down into his bury the ferret is going to have a very difficult job trying to bolt him. The fer-

ret may not succeed and you will probably have a dig that could have been avoided. (You will come to appreciate the seriousness of this every time you are forced to dig. Ferreting is sport, ferreting is fun. Digging is potentially very hard work and best avoided whenever possible.)

Outer layers of clothing, wet or dry, should be dowdy and dull. Army surplus camouflage garments are a good option, helping you to conceal your presence (although you will still need to be quiet and unmoving – camouflage only really works efficiently when you are stationary). Ideally, you should not stand in front of holes either, unless it cannot be avoided. These garments also have the advantage of being readily available and relatively inexpensive.

On your feet, good sturdy boots are the order of the day. Consider buying boots a size or so larger than normal to allow you to wear extra pairs of socks to combat the cold. Wellington boots are acceptable, but you may find them uncomfortable and too sweaty. Hiking boots are an alternative, but they tend to be expensive. Back you go to the army surplus store for some British Army assault boots. The tongue is stitched all the way to the top, so, providing you do not wade through water deeper than the height of the boots, they are waterproof. They are sturdy, lending support to your ankles, which is vital when crossing rough terrain or ploughed fields. Another advantage is that they are probably about half the price of reasonable quality hiking boots.

PURSE NETS

The purse net is basically a sheet of netting with each end gathered and fitted with a metal ring. A draw cord is passed through one ring (the running ring) along one side of the net, through the other ring (the fixed ring) back down the other side of the net, and through the first ring again. This effectively forms a bag with a drawstring closure, like an old-fashioned purse. With the net outstretched, the draw cord extends, on average, 15–30cm beyond the net. The nets come in varying lengths, most commonly 1m long (approximately 3ft 3in), or 1.2m (4ft).

A peg (usually made of softwood, hardwood or plastic) is tied on to the draw cord. I actually staple elastic hairbands to the pegs so that when the nets are wrapped up they can be secured to their peg and not come unfurled in the bag. It is a time-consuming and tiresome task to untangle nets from each other. Brightly coloured hairbands can also help you in finding the nets after use.

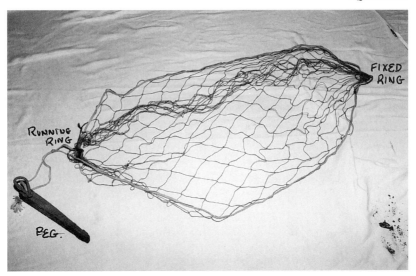

An extended purse net. Note the positions of the fixed ring, running ring and peg.

Traditionally, the nets were made from hemp, but nowadays they are more commonly made from nylon. Hemp nets get wet, gradually becoming heavier as the day goes on, and have to be hung and dried thoroughly after every use to prevent rotting. Nylon nets on the other hand do not absorb water, and are light and efficient. Hemp nets also tend to be about twice the price of nylon. Some people prefer the traditional approach, but others (myself included) prefer nylon, because hemp nets can have a tendency to 'drag', causing a slow closure, and are more prone to pick up debris such as thorns.

Nets are not expensive items to buy, but you can also buy a kit to make your own.

SPADE

The spade is also known as a 'chad' or 'graft'. None of us likes to dig, let's be honest about it. Ferreting is sport, digging is work; depending on the ground, it can be very hard work. But a spade must be included in your equipment just in case it is needed.

Spades vary in shape and size, and also in quality. Choose a spade with a small blade, and buy the best quality that you can.

A good, sturdy spade (above) and a Norfolk long-graft (below).

Some of the work will be hard and there is no point carrying a spade that will break easily.

The best-known spade in ferreting circles is the 'Norfolk long-graft'. Its blade is pointed, and cranked upward in the manner of a shovel. It is also slightly dished. Overall it is about 8ft long, with a hook at the top end of the shaft that can be used to lift a ferret out of a hole by its harness. (I personally believe in recovering ferrets by hand, as greater care may be exercised and the ferrets are less likely to be frightened.)

KNIFE

You will find a use for two knives. A small 'lock-knife' will perform two functions. First, it can be used for the 'hocking and legging' of rabbits (making a small cut between the Achilles tendon and bone of one hind leg, and passing the other hind foot through it to facilitate easy hanging and carrying of dead rabbits). Second, it may be used for paunching the rabbits (removing the stomach and intestines).

The second knife, a sheath knife, is used for any other purposes that require a knife. Its primary use is to probe and loosen soil for about the last six inches of a dig to ensure that the ferret is not injured by a spade crashing through into the tunnel.

FERRET-CARRYING BOX

The ferrets have to be carried to and from the workings and a box is by far the safest method of doing so. Ferret-carrying bags are available, but they are not sufficiently secure. A ferret could easily be injured or killed if someone were to step on the bag. Also, the ferrets will not find it very difficult to escape, should the mood take them – the scent of rabbit is a more than adequate incentive! Use a bag like this to carry nets instead.

Boxes can be bought reasonably inexpensively, but the alternative is to build your own. Use 3mm hardwood exterior plywood, reinforced with bands of 19 × 6mm wood batten around the top, middle and bottom. Use 6 mm square section wood in the corners to join the panels. All joints are held together with PVA exterior wood adhesive and are stapled. Each box holds two ferrets, separated by a dividing panel. Each side has its own sliding lid, secured by a magnetic lock or other form of latch. There is a hinged lid above this that is secured by toggle latches. Air holes are drilled near the top of each section. These holes are best made in the ends of the box, as they are less likely to become blocked off. Holes made in the side are easily obstructed by the carrier's clothing. When finished, the boxes are treated with wood stain and varnish to protect them from the weather.

The carrying strap needs to be wide so as not to cut into your shoulders. Try using an old car seat belt; a sliding buckle arrangement can facilitate adjustment to make carrying more comfortable and safer.

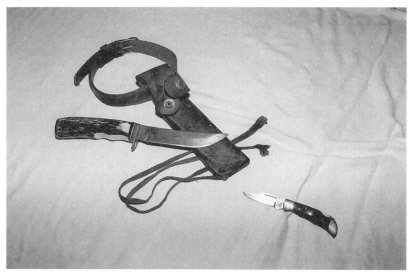

A sheath knife, for probing and so on, and a small lock-knife for paunching and hocking and legging rabbits.

Example of a ferret-carrying box.

EXTRA ITEMS

When considering useful extra items, bear in mind the fact that everything has to be carried. On your return journey, hopefully you will also be burdened by a nice catch of rabbits in addition to your equipment.

Extra items to consider include the following:

- electronic ferret finder;
- long nets or gate nets;
- secateurs;
- gardening gloves;
- kneepads;
- small pick;
- small hatchet;
- machete;
- trowel;
- priest;
- means to carry rabbits.

An array of 'useful tools'.

Electronic Ferret Finder

The electronic ferret finder is a most useful device, although it is not a basic necessity and you can manage without it. It is also quite expensive.

It is a two-part system. First, the leather transmitter collar. This incorporates a small transmitter, sealed in epoxy resin and is powered by a small battery, which hangs under the ferret's neck. (It is designed to operate with silver oxide batteries, and should under no circumstances be used with zinc air types. Such items as hearing aid batteries will cause you to lose your signal.) Collars are available in standard and micro sizes. The micro version is less cumbersome, and less likely to become tangled in a net. There are also two effective range options, 8ft (2.4m) and 15ft (4.5m).

My collars are modified to be used in conjunction with a harness, the ferret is less likely to lose it if it becomes tangled up, for example, in roots. The band of the collar is fitted through a loop in one end of a short leather strap, while another band is fitted through a loop in the other end of the strap. The collar is fitted securely around the ferret's neck. The short strap passes down the ferret's back, between its shoulder blades, and the second band is secured around its chest, making it far more difficult for the ferret to shed its collar.

Two ferret finder receivers (one 8ft and one 15ft) with five collars (all with harness modifications).

Before fitting the collar to the ferret, the battery is installed, and the battery cap is covered and sealed with insulating tape to increase security and prevent water getting in.

The second part of the system is the receiver, powered by a 9-volt battery. It has a rotary disc projecting from one side that is graduated to determine the distance from the collar, and, therefore, from the ferret. The distance is measured in feet. It emits a clicking sound.

To use the finder, you sweep it across the surface of the ground on its maximum setting until a signal is detected. Then you gradually reduce the setting and the area being swept until it is at the minimum level of signal and area of ground. In this way, the position of the ferret is discovered; the dial indicates the distance between the receiver and the collar, in other words, the depth to the ferret.

Long Nets or Gate Nets

Such nets are not usually associated with ferreting. A long net has a top and bottom string and is supported on poles that are pushed into the ground. They vary in length, from around 25yd (23m) to 50yd (45m) or even 100yd (90m). The body of the net hangs like a bag behind the poles. Traditionally the poles were made from well-seasoned hazel wood, but a more modern alternative is fibreglass, or electric-fence posts, which are freely available and have a sturdy metal spike on the bottom that is fairly easily pushed into the ground.

The top and bottom strings are retained securely to the poles and the net is allowed to 'bag' freely. With the net set up and the posts spaced around 3-5yd (3–4m) apart, the strings are fixed as follows: stand facing the net; twist the rubber securing band to the pole; with the string between yourself and the pole, grasp the right-hand string and loop it around the pole anti-clockwise; then take the left-hand string and loop it around the pole clockwise; stretch the rubber securing band over the string and twist it on to the pole on the other side of the string, so that it bridges over the string and secures it positively. The bottom string must obviously be secured prior to setting up poles in the ground.

In the past, the rubber bands were usually cut from old inner tubes. As an alternative, ask the manager at your local swimming pool to order for you some of the coloured rubber wrist or ankle bands that they use in their call-out system for busy sessions. The bands are relatively inexpensive and are intended for use in water, which means they tend to last longer.

A gate net is similar to a long net but much shorter, designed only to span gateways.

Ordinarily the net is set up across the width of a field with large numbers of rabbits on it after dark. The rabbits are frightened or chased into the net, where they become tangled. Someone then walks along the length of the net, picking up the rabbits and despatching them.

In ferreting, the nets are used to surround the perimeter of a bury or mound to act as a 'backstop' to catch any escaping rabbits. They can also be used to surround the perimeter of a mound that is too soft or sandy to be purse netted, where attempts to move on the ground would result in its collapse. They can also be used when working a hedgerow by putting them through the hedge if there is a gap in it. Alternatively, one net can be put on either side of the hedge, projecting into the field, to catch any escaping rabbits that try to evade capture by bolting down the line of the hedge.

Secateurs

A small pair of secateurs is very useful, with so much time spent working under hedges and bushes, with small branches getting in the way and potentially tangling nets. Obstacles are easily and quietly snipped off with the minimum of disturbance that otherwise might alert the occupants of the bury to your presence.

Gardening Gloves and Kneepads

Gardening gloves will protect your hands from thorns, stinging nettles and thistles, and other debris encountered in your endeavours. Including carpet fitter's kneepads in your kit will make crawling around and kneeling on thorns and other debris much more bearable.

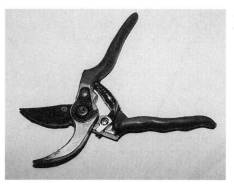

Secateurs pictured open; they can and should be locked shut for safety.

Gardening gloves are essential to protect hands from thorns and other dangers.

Knee pads.

Small Pick

This is an item that will probably not be used very often, but will be worth its weight when it is needed. Should you know the nature of the terrain you are working you may not always need to carry it, but if the ground is particularly hard or you expect to encounter large rocks, for example, it will come in very useful.

Small Hatchet

A hatchet can sometimes be purchased with a sort of holster arrangement that fits to your belt, making carrying less of a problem. As with the pick, this tool will not be needed very often, but if you should have to dig in the vicinity of root complexes it can be most useful.

A small pick.

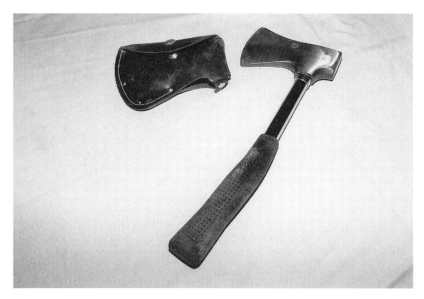

A small hatchet with its holster, designed to be attached to a belt for easier carrying.

Machete

A machete is normally supplied with a scabbard or sheath, allowing it to be suspended from your belt. Carrying is therefore relatively easy, and you will be glad to have it with you where there is the sort of undergrowth and weeds that would otherwise make access to burys either difficult or virtually impossible. Clearing operations are carried out much more quickly with this tool than without it.

Trowel

A trowel is only really useful when you are digging through the last 6in or so of a dig, and you can easily manage without it.

Priest

The priest is a short instrument, weighted at one end. It is used to despatch (kill) prey species. The rabbit is held by its hind legs, head downward, and is struck firmly behind the head, breaking its neck.

Means to Carry Rabbits

This is the one piece of equipment that you will always want to use and there are a number of options.

The first is the most obvious and the one that you will always have with you – your hands. With everything else that you have to carry, however, this option is not always practical.

The second is the easiest to carry when not in use – a simple piece of string, preferably nylon baling twine, which will not absorb water and then rot. If you tie the ends together, making it into a loop, it is then possible to pass the end through the first rabbit's legs (after hocking and legging it), and feed the end of the string through itself, securing the rabbit. The string is then passed through each subsequent hocked and legged rabbit, which slides down alongside the previous one.

The third is a game bag, either made of netting or with large netting panels. The netting is essential for ventilation, to allow the carcasses to cool. If they are not allowed to cool, they will sweat and the meat will be wasted. The bag can also be used to carry some of the equipment.

The fourth option is a long pole, or the handle of a Norfolk longgraft: simply hock and leg the rabbits and slide the pole through their legs. Two people then carry the pole between them.

A machete and scabbard, again designed to be carried on a belt.

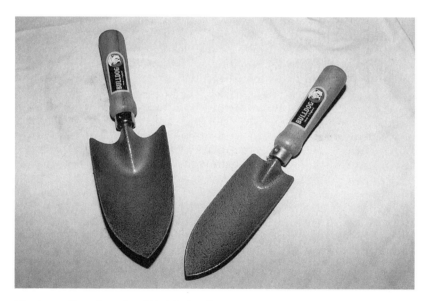

Two types of trowel, one broad-bladed, the other narrow.

8

Obtaining Hunting Rights

As you travel through the countryside, whether by road or on foot along public footpaths, you will certainly see the extent of rabbit damage, but this does not necessarily mean that the landowner will welcome you and your ferrets with open arms. Obtaining the right to hunt can sometimes be very difficult and you will probably have several refusals for every acceptance. Whatever the response to your approach, always take the answer politely and thank the person for their time. You never know, a refusal may turn into an acceptance at a later date.

When you find an area that is rabbit damaged, make enquiries locally and ascertain who owns the relevant land. If possible obtain an introduction from someone on whose land you already have permission if they know the person concerned. Alternatively, once you have the information, look up the telephone number and call the person. Explain to them who you are, and the reason why you are calling. Try to arrange an appointment so that you can meet them.

When you go to meet them, dress tidily and go in a clean car. Carry a pair of wellingtons so that you can change your footwear if necessary. Take an Ordnance Survey map so that you can mark out the boundaries clearly; this way there is no ambiguity about who owns what. If the person you meet is not the landowner, be sure that you do have the *landowner's* permission. The person you meet may farm the land, but if they are renting or leasing it you will need the owner's permission too. If there is a gamekeeper make his acquaintance as soon as possible, first, to make sure that you will recognize each other, and second, so that he can appraise you of the rabbit situation.

If there are buries in boundary hedgerows ask the farmer who owns the adjoining land. Some people believe that it is basically an unwritten rule that you can operate on both sides of a boundary hedge, but it is far better to ask for specific permission. The neighbouring farmer may also have a rabbit problem and you might pick up permission on his land too.

Always try to get your permission in writing. Some farmers are so busy with their work on the land that they do not like to spend time writing letters. You can easily circumvent this problem by offering to write it out and just ask him to sign it when you see him next. Once it is completed, photocopy it and put the original in a safe place. When you are on the land, carry the copy and some form of identification in case you are challenged by anyone.

A simple example of consent would be as follows:

                                Name

                                Address

To whom it may concern,

I hereby grant permission to [your name] to humanely destroy pest species on my land by ferreting, and to remove the kill.

Signed

Name

Position

Once you have the permission, always stay within the agreed boundaries. Never be tempted under any circumstances to cross the border. This would be poaching, and you can guarantee that will lose you permission faster than anything else. A poacher is a thief and no one wants a thief on his or her property.

Always park your car considerately and be sure that it is not in any way going to be a hindrance. Remember, you are going to be away from it for several hours.

Whenever you see the farmer take time to talk with him, without holding him up. He can keep you updated with movements and changes in the area. Listen to anything he says, take in gossip in case it should prove useful to you but never spread it. Never pass on derogatory comments about anyone.

Pay very close attention to everything around you. If he has animals on his land and you find one in difficulties, help it if you can, but make him aware of the situation immediately. If any of his fences are down or damaged, notify him. Should you discover anything suspicious be sure he is aware of it.

When traversing the land either to, from, or between rabbit workings always respect his crops. Stick to public footpaths or walk around the edge of the field. Never mess about or interfere with anything, and if you take anyone else along (particularly children) make sure that they behave in a responsible manner. Remember, it is *your* permission and reputation that are at stake.

9

The Art of Ferreting

Once you have sorted out your equipment and the permission is all in order, it is time to get to the sport. Park up, unload, and go in search of coney.

IDENTIFYING WORKING BURIES

It is quite often possible to identify rabbit buries from some distance away. The first, most obvious sign in arable fields is the rabbit damage. This commonly extends from the hedgerow, where the rabbits are living, in a semicircle out into the field. In severe cases, it may extend into the field for several yards, and from one end of the field to the other.

Another classic sign found in both arable and pasture fields can often be seen from a great distance. Survey the hedges carefully. If you see an area with a prolific growth of stinging nettles, go and investigate. Stinging nettles are among few, if not the only, plants to thrive in ground soaked in rabbit urine.

In the wintertime, when the leaves have fallen, look carefully at the lower levels of hedge growth and small trees for evidence of 'barking'. Hungry rabbits will gnaw the bark off the stems. Rabbit damage will occur just above the ground, normally no more than a foot up. Similar damage higher up will probably have been caused by other animals; a couple of feet up or so, the culprit is most likely deer, and higher than that you will be able to blame squirrels.

Having found your bury it is time to get to grips with the task in hand. The first order of business is to ascertain whether or not it is a working bury and if there is likely to be anyone home! Also, at this point, there is another consideration and a word of warning. As the law stands, it is a criminal offence to interfere with a badger or its set, and it is not unheard of for badgers and rabbits to co-habit. The joint occupancy usually happens when a rabbit has dug its bury, and the badger comes upon the scene and decides to move in.

Classic rabbit damage to a young crop.

Usually it occurs in older workings where the surface openings have widened with long-term use. Indications of possible badger habitation are these large surface openings; obviously, the badger requires a larger tunnel than a rabbit. Other possible indicators are straw dragged into the hole (the badger uses this for bedding)and, if you are particularly fortunate, there will be tracks present, thereby leaving no doubt.

If, after your inspection, you are still not sure whether or not badgers are present, err on the side of caution and leave well alone. Move on to another working. It is your legal obligation and duty to abide by the laws of the land and countryside – and if your ferret should encounter a badger, the ferret would probably stand very little chance in a conflict.

Smell the area. Often, busy workings have a distinct aroma that you will learn to recognize with experience. In the past, I have detected a working rabbit bury by smell from 15ft or more away. Look at the holes carefully for signs of use. Common indications are things like tracks, trodden-down leaves in entrances, blades of grass or other vegetation that have been trailed into the hole as the rabbit has gone to ground, and fresh droppings.

Above: Much less severe damage, although the rabbits have not stopped when they have eaten the lush, green tops. They have continued to gnaw away at the root crop in the ground!

Gnawed tubers.

Typical rabbit territory: rabbit-damaged crop in the foreground and a prolific growth of stinging nettles behind, the rabbits' home!

There are two types of rabbit droppings, first and second motions. Because the food passes through the rabbit's digestive system fairly quickly, all the available nutrition is not absorbed and would therefore go to waste. To remedy this the rabbit generally eats its first motions as it passes them, although sometimes it passes them to the ground. The difference is usually fairly obvious. First motions normally have a greener colouring and are moister than second motions, which tend to be darker or blacker and harder.

The presence of fresh droppings, particularly first motions, usually indicates an active bury. It does not however guarantee that it is inhabited at this particular point in time, as the inhabitants may be out feeding.

Survey the area carefully and quietly. Be sure to walk as softly as possible, as your footsteps will transmit as vibrations through the ground, and the rabbit can either hear these or feel them with its whiskers. Something as simple and quiet to us as a twig breaking is a sizeable sonic crack to a rabbit and a grand announcement of your presence.

TRADITIONAL FERRETING WITH NETS

In this endeavour the holes are covered with purse nets to capture the rabbit as it tries to make good its escape from the ferret.

Netting the Area

Look especially carefully for bolt-holes, openings that are obviously too small for a rabbit to pass through as you see them. They appear to be more likely to be rat, mouse or other small vermin holes, but in reality what you are seeing is a small opening at the end of a rabbit's escape tunnel. If it is being chased, the rabbit can run into this remaining thin layer of earth, explode on to the surface, and disappear across the scenery. The safest approach is, if in doubt, net it.

Clear away any debris that you can from in and around the holes. Unwrap your purse net carefully and push the peg firmly into the ground behind the entrance to the hole. Be careful not to push it through into the tunnel. If for some reason you cannot secure the

A correctly set purse net. Note the position of the peg, running ring and fixed ring. The running ring is free to slide or 'run' along the draw cord, the fixed ring is pushed firmly into or 'fixed' in the ground.

peg in the ground and there is a suitable branch nearby, wrap the end of the draw cord around the branch and tie the net to it by slipping the peg through, between the two sides of the draw cord. Be sure that it is secure. Hold the other end of the drawstring by the 'fixed ring' and lay the net carefully over the hole, with one side of the drawstring on either side of the hole. Push the fixed ring into the ground in front of the hole. If the sides of the net persistently fall into the hole it is possible to restrain them by either pushing the drawstring into the earth gently, or securing it with *small* stones. Make sure that whatever you do will not impede the net's closure or you may lose a rabbit that would otherwise have been caught.

Entering the Ferrets

Once all of the holes are netted in this manner, and the perimeter net has been erected if it is being used, you are now ready to enter the ferret(s). Make sure that everyone has some spare nets in their pockets. Select the ferrets to be used and ensure that their collars and harness arrangements, if used, are secure. Test the transmitters to be sure that they are working (as described on page 40). When all is

An albino ferret being entered to a bury.

well, give the ferrets a drink of saliva from the palm of your hand, and stroke them gently. Lift the side of a net and enter each ferret in a different hole, if possible at opposite ends of the bury. Once a ferret is seen to go down, notify your companions, usually by saying quietly 'ferret in the hole'. Check the time.

Now all you can do is wait. Watch attentively, looking not only for bolting rabbits, but also for ferrets. Knowing where your ferrets are as much as possible can save time with the locator, if you have to use it. If you see the ferret go past a hole indicate to the other members of the team and show its direction. Also watch out for the possibility of the ferret surfacing where you have no net. It is always possible that you have missed a hole. Should this occur, net the hole quickly and quietly.

If a ferret comes up, wait for it to walk out of the hole a short distance before attempting to pick it up. If possible put your hand on the ground, palm upwards, and let it walk on to it. Pick it up as usual (*see* page 37). Examine the ferret for signs of blood or fur on

The preferred method of despatching a rabbit (the rabbit used for this photograph was already dead).

its hands and face. Make sure that it is not injured. Enter it into another hole.

When a rabbit bolts, act quickly. Grab it as rapidly as you can to make sure that it does not get free. Place your foot over the hole to ensure that if another rabbit should try to bolt through here that it cannot escape through the un-netted hole. Either give the rabbit to someone to despatch while you re-net the hole, or allow someone else to re-net and despatch the rabbit yourself.

Rabbits must be despatched as quickly as possible to avoid suffering and cruelty. There are a number of ways to achieve this:

1. Hold the rabbit by its hind legs, head downwards, and 'chop' it, karate-style, behind the head, breaking its neck. This method often results in bruising of the shoulders, making the meat appear unsightly.
2. Hold the rabbit in a similar manner and strike it behind the head with a priest, again breaking its neck. This method can also cause bruising of the shoulders, and a priest is just another item to carry.
3. Hold the rabbit's hind legs in one hand, and grasp it securely around the head with the other, index finger under the jaw and thumb around the head, just behind the ears. Turn its head backwards, as if making it look up, and pull your hands in opposite directions firmly, breaking its neck.

The rabbit will often twitch, and sometimes even kick for several minutes after death. Do not be concerned about this. The movements are involuntary nerve pulses. The animal is dead. If you want to be 100 per cent certain for your own peace of mind you can perform a simple test. Hold the rabbit by its head and touch its eye with your finger. There should be no response.

Continue in this manner until you feel sure that you have caught all the rabbits that there are to catch. Withdraw the ferrets and give them a drink of saliva. Stroke them and talk to them gently to calm them down if they appear to be 'hotted up'. Remove as much hair and dirt from their hands and feet as possible. Examine them for any signs of injuries sustained and return them to their boxes.

Digging Out Ferrets

In the event of a ferret not returning to the surface, you will have to discover its position and dig it out. This can happen for a number of reasons. Whatever the reason, if you are on grass, carefully cut a section of the turf and set it to one side. When the dig is over, refill the hole and reposition the turf patch on the top. Tread it down well. Wherever you dig, always refill the hole and tread it down firmly, making good any damage. Always endeavour to leave the place as you found it … with the obvious exception of a reduced rabbit population!

The first reason for digging is that the ferret could be trapped. It may have got over the top of a rabbit in a 'blind stop' (a tunnel that comes to an end underground) in an attempt to move it. In its attempts to move the rabbit it might possibly have killed it and as a result become trapped. Another way that it could have become trapped is if it is in a position out of which it simply cannot climb.

The second reason is that it could be in what is called a 'lie up'. This is when it has killed a rabbit, eaten its fill, and is sleeping it off. If ferrets are properly kept and fed, this should not occur. Some say that a ferret should be starved for a day or two before working it, but my personal feelings are that this will not only cause them to tire more easily, but is also more likely to lead to a lie up. If the ferrets are hungry they will naturally eat if they get the chance. Having said this, the ferrets should not be fed immediately prior to working, as they would be prone to sleeping off their meal, consequently causing lie ups and digs. Feed ferrets in the evening to avoid this potential problem.

The third reason is that if the ferret has trapped a rabbit, but is unable to move it, it could be marking it for you to dig it out. This may sound unlikely, but I have a jill who will quite often do it. On one occasion I had to dig down to her three times on the same bury! The first time, as I broke through into the tunnel she moved off. I extracted and despatched the trapped rabbits, and netted the hole. I tracked her down with the locator and dug to her again. As I broke through she disappeared, again leaving rabbits to be dealt with. Having netted this hole, I tracked her down yet again and dug for a third time. This time she waited until I had broken through, looked up, and, as I reached down, climbed straight on to my hand for extraction. Again there were rabbits. Digging three times on the same bury, for the same ferret, was thought to be exceptional, but there were rabbits every time. Fortunately, the digging was easy and each dig was only about 2ft deep. This is a perfect example of the benefit of having and using the electronic ferret finder. Without it, there would have been fewer rabbits in the bag, and probably a very long wait for her to resurface. After clearing all of the equipment from the bury the holes that I had made were all backfilled and trodden down firmly.

A net being cleared of debris. Note also the
effectiveness of camouflage clothing.

'Peeing' a rabbit.

The fourth possibility is one that none of us wants: that the ferret may have met its match and be lying seriously injured or even dead.

Collecting Nets

Ferrets recovered, you can now set about the collection of the nets. It is good practice to count the nets as you set them so that you know how many you have to recover afterwards. Not only is it expensive if you continually leave nets behind, it is also irresponsible and dangerous to wildlife. This sort of behaviour is not to be tolerated in the countryside.

Go to each net in turn, lift the fixed ring and hold it away from the peg. Clean all the debris out of the net. Slide the running ring as far along the draw cord as possible from the fixed ring and withdraw the peg from the ground. Clean it. Fold the fixed ring to the running ring and smooth the net. Fold the end of the net to the rings. Smooth the net again and repeat the last fold. Wrap the remaining draw cord around the net and secure the two together by pulling the elastic hairband (if used) over the net. Bag it. It is now ready to be used again.

Dealing with the Dead Rabbits

The dead rabbits should be left laid out on the ground, not piled up, as this will retain body heat and spoil the meat. After the rabbits have been allowed to rest for five minutes or so to relax, they must be 'peed'. This is the removal of urine from the bladder which, if left, could also spoil the meat.

Bend over, holding the rabbit, head uppermost, with its belly facing away from you. With its back in your hands, place your thumbs just below its ribcage on the abdomen. Press your thumbs towards the animal's spine and slide them downwards towards its tail, maintaining the pressure in the direction of the spine. A steady stream of urine should be ejected.

Hock and leg the rabbits (*see* page 47) ready to transport them. You now have two choices: you can take the rabbits with you, but as their number increases they will become a very heavy load. Alternatively you could begin your day's sport by walking out examining prospective workings on the way, start at an outermost point, and then work back towards the vehicles. This way, you will not have to carry rabbits out, just to carry them back again. The alternative is, assuming that you will return along the same route, to build 'rabbit nests'. This involves hanging or lodging them in a tree, to be collected on your return. If you should opt for this choice be sure that you place them high, and securely enough, to prevent other predators such as foxes from taking them. You will not be pleased if you arrive to pick them up and find that a fox, for example, has already collected them.

At the end of your day's sport, all the rabbits must be paunched. Dig a decent hole, at least 2ft deep. Take a sharp knife and make a small cut in the abdomen of the rabbit just below the sternum (the bone down the centre of the chest, joining the ribs). Insert your index and second fingers either side of the knife blade to prevent the knife puncturing the intestines, and slide the knife down the abdomen, opening the cavity. Hold the rabbit over the hole and turn it over so that the back is uppermost. Shake it to displace the entrails and stomach. Pull the stomach and bowel from their respective attachments and deposit them in the hole. When all of the rabbits have been done, refill the hole and tread it down firmly.

SHOOTING OVER FERRETS

An alternative sport, preferred by some, and potentially more exciting, is 'shooting over ferrets'. In this endeavour, a suitable vantage point is occupied by a person or persons armed with shotguns. When prepared, the ferrets are entered to the workings. The rabbits bolt to escape the ferrets, and are shot as they flee. It is essential to give the rabbit a reasonable lead away from the hole to ensure that the ferret is not attached so as to prevent it being injured.

There are disadvantages to this option. The noise of the guns can frighten the ferrets, possibly making them skulky, and there may be damage to their hearing. Also the rabbits can be peppered with shotgun pellets, making their eating less pleasurable.

After collecting the kill, the rabbits must be peed and paunched as described previously.

If you should choose to try this, remember that above all safety is paramount. Safe gun-handling practices must be strictly adhered to at all times. Accidents can happen at any time, but with high levels of excitement their occurrence is all the more likely. Consequently they must be guarded against much more carefully.

GOING HOME

Carry a sheet of plastic or a couple of large dustbin bags to spread out in the back of the car so that any dirt from the equipment can be easily removed. These also serve to protect the upholstery from any blood that may leak from the rabbits.

Having lined the interior, load your equipment into the car first, followed by the rabbits. If there is room, transport the ferrets on the back seat. If you do need to carry them in the back, make sure that the box is stable and that nothing heavy can fall onto it. The ferrets will not benefit from being buffeted about.

Having arrived home and unloaded the car, the next thing is to tend to the ferrets. Take them from the boxes and remove their collars and harnesses. Give them a drink from your hand and examine them thoroughly for any injuries or signs of ticks that they may have picked up while out. Assuming all is well, return them to their cages or courts and feed them. Remove the batteries from the collars and put them away until needed again. Once the ferrets have been taken care of you can start to think of yourself. Wash your hands and put the kettle on.

—— 10 ——
Dressing the Kill

If you do not intend to prepare the rabbits immediately, you can hang them by the hind legs somewhere cold, but it is advisable to attend to them as soon as possible.

If you are dressing them on the kitchen table or worktop, cover the surface with some newspaper to facilitate easier cleaning up afterwards. Take a good sturdy board (a small offcut of kitchen worktop serves well) and place it on top of the papers to use as a work surface or butcher's block. Line a bucket with a plastic carrier bag to receive the waste and have a basin to hand for the offal.

SKINNING

There are two ways of skinning rabbits, depending on whether you want to keep and use the skins or not.

Disposing of the Skins

Take the rabbit and place it on its back on the board. Starting at the incision previously made for paunching, separate the skin from the peritoneum (the membrane that retains the contents of the abdomen) and bluntly dissect it all the way around to the back of the animal. Push the hind legs, one at a time, up and forward out of their skin. As soon as you can get a finger in behind the knee joint, do so, and pull the skin down the leg to the ankle. The skin may tear off at this point; alternatively, cut around it and pull the foot through. Repeat this for the other hind leg.

Pull the skin off the tail, and peel it forwards. It should now be free as far as the ribcage. Take the hind legs in one hand and the skin in the other, and pull firmly in opposite directions, peeling the skin off as far as the neck. Push the front legs up and back out of their skin, in the same manner as the hind legs, as far as the wrist. The skin may tear off at this point; otherwise, cut around it and pull the legs through.

Peel the skin up as far as the base of the skull and sever the head. Drop the skin and head in the waste receptacle. Sever the feet at the ankles and the 'hands' at the wrists and dispose of them in the same way.

Retaining the Skins

Skins are suitable for keeping only when the rabbit has completed its moult, otherwise the hair will drop out continually until the skin is bald.

Take a rabbit and place it on the board as before on its back. Extend the paunching incision forwards, as far as the base of the head, and backwards to the tail. Cut the skin outwards from this incision down the inside of the hind legs to the ankle and down the inside of the front legs to the wrists. Assuming that you do not wish

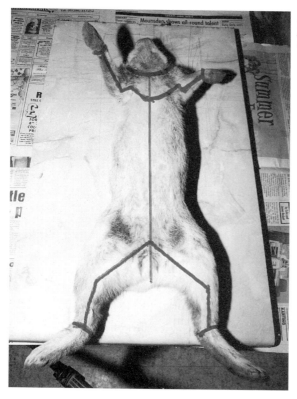

Approximate positions for skinning incisions, should you wish to retain the pelt.

to keep the hands and feet on the skin, cut around the limbs at this point. Again, assuming that you do not wish to skin the head, cut around the neck at the base of the skull. The skin can now be bluntly dissected from the body. Sever the hands, feet and head and dispose of them in the waste receptacle.

The skin must be dried or cured to prevent decomposition. There are various methods for carrying out this process, and it is advisable to refer to relevant material before attempting this.

CLEANING OUT AND JOINTING

Once the skinning is complete, it is time to clean out the internals. Remove the liver, kidneys, diaphragm (membrane that controls breathing and separates the chest and abdominal cavities), lungs and heart. Examine the liver for signs of liver fluke (white specks). If there are any signs, discard it. Otherwise, remove the gall bladder from the liver and dispose of it in the waste, and place the liver in the basin with the other offal. Clean any remaining waste tissue such as the anus and, in the case of bucks, the penis, etc., and wash and dry the body.

A rabbit liver on a plate, showing the position of the gall bladder (ringed in white).

Joint the body as follows: remove the peritoneum by cutting down behind the ribs, along the side of the back muscles, and down between the legs. This can be added to the offal for feeding to the ferrets.

Feel along the top of the hind legs until you find the top of the pelvis, cut backwards from here to the hip joint. Flex the leg outwards, dislocating the hip, and sever the leg. Repeat this operation on the other hind leg.

Cut or chop through the back behind the ribcage. To portion for cooking, cut this in front of the pelvis and divide the back or 'saddle' according to requirements.

Turn the ribcage and shoulders over. Cut through the meat to the spine and pare it around the ribs to remove the front legs and shoulders. The ribcage and neck can be put with the offal for the ferret food. The pelvis can also go with the ferret food as it generally has too little meat to be of use in meals.

Jointing the rabbit in this manner makes for easy bagging 'flat-pack' style for freezing, and also creates convenient portions for cooking.

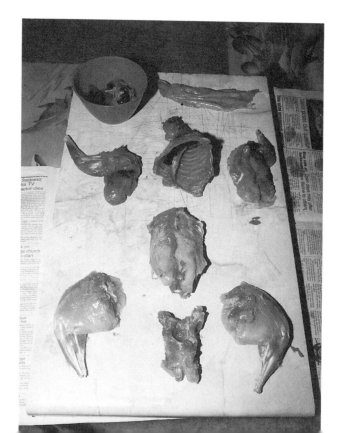

A jointed rabbit.

— 11 —

To the Table

In my opinion, freshly caught wild food is delicious. Animals that are wild live by their wits and cannot afford to carry superfluous amounts of fat. If they did they would soon be on the menu of a predator. As a result, the meat of a wild animal is lean and healthy, and the flavour of wild-caught food is far superior to that of farmed, intensively grown alternatives. In addition it has the benefit of being far less expensive, and a good day's sport can be enjoyed in obtaining it.

Below are some ideas on how to use the rabbits you catch. It is not necessary to follow the recipes to the letter; any quantities given are approximate and intended as a guideline. Cook by feel and according to your individual taste.

Eat and enjoy.

BUNNY BURGERS

Two good rabbits
One medium onion (finely diced)
Five sage leaves
One egg
One chicken stock cube
Tomato purée
Worcestershire sauce
Freshly ground black pepper
Three rashers of rindless streaky bacon

Fillet the meat from the bones of the rabbits (the bones can be added to a stock pot and boiled for use elsewhere). Mince the rabbit meat and bacon finely and add the diced onion. Finely chop the sage leaves, and add the herb and the crumbled stock cube to the rabbit mix in a suitable mixing bowl. Add the tomato purée, Worcestershire sauce and freshly ground black pepper according to taste, and mix thoroughly. Beat the egg and add it to the mixture to help bind it together. Mix it all.

Form burger patties from the mixture. They should not be too thick, otherwise they will take too long to cook through properly and the outsides will become burnt and dry. Form the patties either manually or in a burger press, but make sure they are packed together firmly so that they do not disintegrate during cooking.

Fry in a pan in a little olive oil for a few minutes each side until cooked through. Serve in bread rolls with salad, relish and cheese if desired, accompanied by a portion of chipped potatoes.

RICH RABBIT PIE

Two good rabbits
Twelve shallots
100g (4oz) button mushrooms
75g (3oz) chestnut mushrooms (quartered)
Two cloves garlic
One bottle red wine
50g (2oz) rindless smoked bacon
1 tsp fresh chopped sage
Two bay leaves
75g (3oz) butter
1 dsp English mustard
1 tbsp tomato purée
Worcestershire sauce
Black pepper
Puff pastry

Joint the rabbits as previously described. If they are not particularly young, they will probably benefit from being marinated overnight in the red wine, prior to cooking.

Brown the rabbit joints in the butter and remove them from the pan; set aside to keep warm. Slice the shallots and bacon and cook in the pan until the shallots are soft. Add the mushrooms and cook for a further few minutes. Return the rabbit to the pan. Add the tomato purée, crushed garlic, mustard and red wine. Raise the heat until the pan is just simmering, then reduce the heat to maintain the simmer. Add the sage and bay leaves, Worcestershire sauce and black pepper to taste. Leave to simmer gently for one and a half to two hours, stirring occasionally, until the meat is cooked through and tender. Remove from the heat and leave to cool.

When it is cold, remove the bay leaves and discard. Remove the rabbit from the pan and separate the meat from the bones. Discard the bones, and return the meat to the pot, mix it in well.

You now have two options. Put the meat filling in a suitably sized pie dish, cover with the pastry, brush with beaten egg, and bake in a hot oven (200°C) for twenty-five to thirty minutes, until risen and golden. Alternatively, the filling can be distributed into individual-sized pie dishes. The pastry tops should be cut to the required size and baked separately on baking parchment after brushing with egg, in a hot oven as before. They will rise much more efficiently. Once cooked they can either be sealed to the dishes with beaten egg and reheated, also cooking the egg, prior to serving, or the tops can simply be placed on the dishes after reheating. This method will give a much more professional appearance to the dish.

The pie or pies should be served with potatoes and a selection of fresh vegetables.

CONEY KIEV

One young rabbit
275ml ($^1/_2$ pint) cream
Six cloves of garlic
50g (2oz) unsalted butter
Handful fresh parsley
Freshly ground black pepper

Joint the rabbit as previously described, and finely chop the parsley. Melt the butter in a saucepan and gently fry the rabbit to seal it. Remove the meat and place in an ovenproof casserole dish, keeping it warm.

Peel and crush the garlic into the pan of butter and cook it very gently, taking care not to let it burn, as this will make it bitter. Add the cream and parsley, stirring continuously. Season to taste. Pour the sauce over the rabbit, and cover the dish. Place in a medium oven, at about 150°C, and cook gently for about 45 minutes, or until thoroughly cooked and tender.

Serve with creamed potatoes and peas.

RABBIT IN MUSTARD SAUCE

One young rabbit
275ml ($^1/_2$ pint) cream
1 tbsp wholegrain mustard
50g (2oz) unsalted butter
2 rashers of smoked streaky bacon

Prepare and joint the rabbit as previously described.

Melt the butter and gently fry the rabbit meat to seal it. Place it in an ovenproof casserole dish, lay the streaky bacon over it and cover the dish. Roast in a medium oven, at at about 150°C, for 45 minutes, or until thoroughly cooked and tender.

Pour the butter into a saucepan, add the mustard, and pour in the cream, stirring continuously. Cook steadily until the sauce thickens. Serve the rabbit with creamed potatoes and peas. Pour the sauce over the rabbit and garnish with sprigs of mint if desired.

CONEY CHASSEUR

One young rabbit
50g (2oz) seasoned flour
50g (2oz) unsalted butter
4 shallots
100g (4oz) chestnut mushrooms
1 tbsp tomato purée
275ml ($^1/_2$ pint) cream
1 glass medium white wine
Freshly ground black pepper

Prepare and joint the rabbit as previously described. Coat it with the seasoned flour. Melt the butter and gently fry the rabbit meat to seal it. Place it in an ovenproof casserole dish and keep warm.

Slice the shallots and cook in the butter until soft, but not coloured. Slice the mushrooms, add to the pan and shake or stir gently until they take on some colour. Add the tomato purée and the wine and cook until reduced by about one-third. Stir in the cream and raise to a simmer. Season to taste and pour over the rabbit portions. Cover the dish and cook for about 45 minutes or until thoroughly cooked and tender.

Serve with creamed potatoes and vegetables, garnished with a sprinkling of finely chopped parsley if desired.

RABBIT CURRY

2 rabbits
3 good onions
2 large carrots
3 apples
2 potatoes
50g (2oz) sultanas
6 cloves garlic
Curry powder
825ml ($1^1/_2$ pints) good chicken stock
50g (2oz) butter
2 tbsp tomato purée
75g (3oz) seasoned flour
1 tbsp mango chutney

Portion the rabbits as previously described. Wash and dry them, and coat in the seasoned flour.

Roughly chop the onions and grate the carrots with a coarse grater. Peel and core the apples and peel the potatoes. Dice the apples and potatoes.

Melt the butter in a large saucepan and fry the onions and carrots until the onions are beginning to soften. Add the curry powder to taste, then add the rabbit portions. Cook until the meat is beginning to brown. Add the apples and potatoes and cook for a further few minutes, turning the mix over continuously to prevent burning. Stir in any remaining seasoned flour and cook for about two minutes. Pour in the stock, stirring continuously.

Crush the garlic and add it and the tomato purée to the pan. Simmer gently for at least an hour, or until the meat is tender. Add the sultanas for the last fifteen minutes of cooking time. When cooked, stir in the mango chutney.

If desired, thicken the sauce with cornflour slaked with a small amount of water. Alternatively, thickening can be achieved with the use of some gravy granules.

Serve on a bed of boiled rice.

Note: As with all curries it is better to make this one at least twenty-four hours before serving. This allows it to rest and the flavour to improve. Reheating must be done over a low heat, stirring frequently, to avoid burning.

RABBIT IN CIDER

Two rabbits
50g (2oz) seasoned flour
2 tsp fresh sage (finely chopped)
2 sprigs thyme
1 clove garlic
2 medium onions
2 carrots, sliced
1 litre dry cider
1 tbsp tomato purée
50g (2oz) butter
Worcestershire sauce
Freshly ground black pepper

Portion the rabbits as previously described. Wash and dry the portions and coat with the flour. Melt the butter in a pan. Fry the portions gently in the butter to seal them until they are lightly coloured. Remove them from the pan and set aside to keep warm.

Peel and finely chop the onions. Cook in the butter along with the sliced carrots until the onions are soft and beginning to brown. Add the tomato purée and pour in the cider. Raise the heat until just simmering. Add the herbs and crush the garlic into the pan. Return the rabbit portions to the pan and season to taste with the Worcestershire sauce and black pepper. Cook for about one hour or until the meat is tender. When cooked, the gravy can be thickened with cornflour if desired.

Serve with boiled potatoes and peas. Garnish with a sprinkling of fresh finely chopped parsley, and a sprig of fresh mint to complement the potatoes.

— 12 —

Health and Welfare

The subject of ferret illnesses and diseases is a very large one, and a detailed review is beyond the scope of this book. There are many other books about the relevant topics, which may be borrowed from libraries, or ordered and bought from your local bookshop. Another factor to be considered is that, even if it is possible for a layperson to make an accurate diagnosis, access to the necessary drugs and medicines is still not possible. A veterinary surgeon should therefore be consulted in any case.

Having said that, it is the responsibility of any animal keeper to learn as much as possible about the health and welfare of his or her charges. It is essential to examine your ferrets thoroughly on a daily basis. This can easily be done, at feeding time for example, and it does not take long. If the ferrets are kept communally, or have recently been mated, particular attention should be given to the area around the neck and ears, in case bites have penetrated the skin. Any puncture wounds should be bathed with warm salty water to cleanse them and, it is hoped, prevent infection.

Watch how the ferrets move and examine them thoroughly. Remember that ferrets are extremely hardy creatures and rarely display signs of illness until the problem is well advanced. This obviously makes it more difficult to treat, thereby reducing the chances of a full recovery. If there is any cause for concern, make an appointment to take the ferret to a vet as soon as possible.

I would always advise anyone to choose a veterinary practitioner very carefully. Investigations can and should be made prior to the need for consultation so that you know exactly which vet to contact to get the best possible care for your ferret. Not all vets are particularly conversant with ferrets. The best way to find vets that are well experienced in dealing with ferrets is to try to find out if there is a ferret club of any kind in your area. They will tell you which vet they use. If this option is not available, then you will have to use a more direct approach. Locate the veterinary practices in your area and either telephone or visit them. Ask them if they have treated ferrets and, if so, how much experience they have relating to ferrets.

Below is an overview of some of the more common complaints found in ferrets, along with their clinical presentation in order that you will have some point of reference when examining your ferrets.

ABSCESSES

Abscesses generally begin as a wound, which becomes infected and then fills with pus. The most common site is in or around the neck. There are a number of possible causes; bites, sustained during fights, play or mating, and damage to the inside of the mouth or throat by sharp objects such as bones in their food, are probably the most likely.

Clinical presentation is a swelling or lump.

Treatment is usually by lancing or surgically removing the problem, identifying and rectifying the cause, and treating the animal with a course of broad-spectrum antibiotics.

ACTINOMYCOSIS

This is a hardening and swelling of the ferret's oesophagus. It is thought to be precipitated by the feeding of too many day-old chicks, causing abrasions within the oesophagus.

Clinical presentation is a swollen and hard neck, anorexia, listlessness and fever.

The veterinary surgeon will treat the animal by giving injections, and you will need to feed it on a liquid diet until it is recovered.

ALEUTIAN DISEASE

Although not particularly common, this disease is contagious and fatal. It gets its name from the Aleutian strain of mink, in which it was first discovered in the USA during the 1950s. It is an immune deficiency disease, caused by a parvovirus. It can be passed from mother to offspring, or between ferrets in bodily fluids. This need not be the result of physical contact; an infected ferret coughing or sneezing can pass it on. The aerosol droplets resulting from this action can transmit the disease to others up to a metre away.

Clinical presentations include weight loss, lethargy, rear leg weakness, anorexia, tarry faeces, intermittent head tremor, diarrhoea, faecal and urinary incontinence, aggressiveness, fevers.

Ultimately, unless the animal is the subject of euthanasia, it will die. There is no specific treatment, no cure, and no vaccine.

ALOPECIA

This is hair loss, which may be localized, or over the entire animal. It can occur in animals of any gender or any age, and for a number of reasons. These include the feeding of too many raw eggs, the presence of mites, nervous reaction, or just excessive moult.

Clinical presentation obviously is lack of hair.

It is essential to consult a vet, who will examine the ferret, take skin scrapings if necessary for analysis, and treat the animal accordingly.

BITES AND STINGS

Ferrets can suffer bites from a number of sources: from other ferrets during play or more likely in the breeding season, or from snakes, rats or other predators while out working. Other possibilities include bites or stings from insects.

Clinical presentation is a lump or perforation of the ferret's skin.

A small amount of hair or fur should be clipped from the immediate vicinity of the wound. Careful examination should be made to ensure that there is no foreign body or material present in the wound. If anything is discovered it must be removed carefully with tweezers. The wound should then be bathed with a strong saline solution and treated with antiseptic.

Note: if the wound is around the throat, it may be necessary to seek veterinary advice. Should the site swell, it might cause a life-threatening occlusion of the airways.

BOTULISM

Botulism is probably one of the most prevalent killers of ferrets, and is so easily preventable. It is caused by a bacterium, namely

Clostridium botulinum. In the event of this bacteria coming into contact with decaying flesh, a deadly toxin results. Should this 'food' then be ingested, botulism is contracted. It attacks the ferret's nervous system.

Clinical presentation is usually paralysis, commonly originating in the hindquarters and spreading to the vital organs, causing death.

There is no cure for this disease. Prevention is the only defence; this is why great care must be taken to ensure that any remnants of uneaten food are removed from the ferrets' environment.

BROKEN TEETH

Ferrets can fairly easily break or damage their teeth while out working, and this can also be a result of biting or chewing things within their home environment.

Clinical presentation is easily visible, however, your attention may first be attracted by the ferret apparently exhibiting difficulty in eating normally. It may be chewing on one side or displaying discomfort during eating. In severe cases, which should never occur as the problem should be identified early during regular examinations, weight loss will be apparent.

Veterinary attention must be sought.

CANCER

Ferrets can be prone to suffer from cancer, which is potentially fatal. It is not contagious and, if diagnosed early enough, can be surgically treated.

Clinical presentations are usually lumps or swellings on the body of the ferret, or solid internal masses detected by palpation. In cases of gastric carcinoma, for example, in its advanced stages, the ferret will become lethargic and weak, appetite will be lost, and on occasions when food is taken, it will be vomited back shortly afterwards. I particularly mention gastric carcinoma because I am led to believe that it is not uncommon in ferrets.

If suspected, veterinary attention must be sought as early as possible, and advice taken. In advanced cases, euthanasia will probably be recommended.

CANINE DISTEMPER

This is a virus that ferrets are particularly prone to contract. It is fatal. The incubation period is seven to nine days, and dogs are the most likely source of infection. The disease is highly contagious, and as soon as it is suspected the affected animals must be isolated or quarantined. It is only treatable in its early stages, and it is often better to terminate the affected animals once the diagnosis is confirmed.

Clinical presentations are as follows: a rash on the chin; the skin surrounding the lips and chin swelling and becoming crusty, often accompanied by dermatitis on the anus, photophobia, anorexia, depression, swollen feet, followed by the pads hardening, runny eyes and nose, reduction in appetite, increased thirst, and diarrhoea. If the animal is not the subject of euthanasia, it may well vomit, suffer convulsions and become comatose prior to death.

CANKER

The same mite that causes the infection in cats and dogs causes canker of the ears in ferrets. A common cause of cross-infection is ferrets and dogs travelling in close proximity to one another, in a car, on the way to a day's rabbiting.

Clinical presentations are drowsiness, possibly lethargy, reduction of and sometimes a loss of appetite. These symptoms are accompanied by a discharge of wax from the ear(s).

Veterinary consultation is imperative, particularly in the case of young ferrets, as it can lead to meningitis with fatal consequences.

CATARACTS

This condition is seen very frequently in ferrets. The affected animal feels no pain, and manages remarkably well considering that it has lost its sight. This may be partly because the ferret's eyesight is not particularly good anyway, and partly because its working environment is in pitch-dark underground tunnels. Ferrets normally rely mainly on their ears, nose and whiskers for the gathering of sensory information.

Clinical presentation is opacity and cloudiness of the eyes, on examination.

A jill ferret with cataracts, most visible in her left eye, as the cloudy or opaque region.

There is no surgical treatment available, and, as long as the ferret is comfortable and manages to live with quality of life, it should be allowed to continue to do so.

EAR MITES

These pests infest the ears. Unfortunately, they are common in ferrets, and if they migrate down the aural canal they could cause the middle ear to become infected. They are not visible to the naked eye, and an otoscope is required to see them.

Clinical presentation includes head shaking, ear scratching, walking with the head tilted to one side, staggers or balance problems, and a thick brown waxy discharge.

A vet must be consulted, and the animal will be treated with a course of injections, or eardrops. All animals that have been in con-

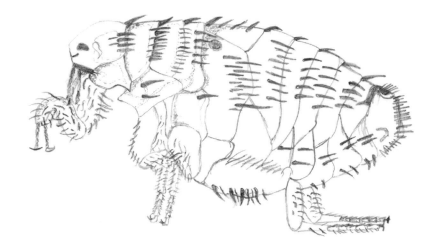

Fleas are parasites that, if allowed, will inhabit the coat of the ferret, making its life a misery.

tact with the affected one must also be treated. All bedding materials and cage litter must be removed and burned and replaced with fresh, otherwise the problem will recur. Under no circumstances should an untrained person attempt to clean anything but the outermost parts of the ears as damage can easily be done.

FLEAS

When the ferret has fleas, clinical presentation is usually excessive scratching, hair loss, and possibly blood spots in the coat.

Treatment is the same as for cats. Buy a product such as Frontline from your vet, spray a small amount on to a rubber glove and stroke it thoroughly into the ferret's coat. All animals that come into contact with the affected individual must also be treated, and the bedding and domicile litter burned and replaced with fresh to prevent recurrence of the problem. The cage or court should be treated with a suitable pesticide.

Note: pregnant or nursing jills in particular should not be treated due to the risk of harming or killing the offspring.

GASTRO-INTESTINAL FOREIGN BODIES

These are abnormal objects inside the animal's intestines, causing a blockage. In young ferrets they are most likely to be pieces of sponge or rubber torn or chewed from their toys; this is why any toys or items supplied for the amusement of ferrets must be selected very carefully. In older ferrets the obstruction is more likely to be caused by tricobezoars (hair balls, *see* page 95), accumulated most often during the ferret's moulting period.

Clinical presentations are lethargy, reduced appetite, anorexia, diarrhoea, vomiting, nausea and weakness. Sometimes the obstruction can be palpated by *gently* examining the animal's abdomen. Quite often X-rays are necessary for confirmation.

Occasionally small obstructions can be induced to pass naturally with the use of intestinal lubricants such as cat laxatives. More commonly, surgical removal is required. Generally recovery is quite rapid. As ever, prevention is far better than cure.

GINGIVITIS

This is a gum disorder, which may lead to loss of teeth or further infections.

Clinical presentation includes 'angry', inflamed gums, and bad breath. The ferret exhibiting difficulty in eating, as with broken teeth, may attract your attention.

Veterinary advice must be sought.

HEATSTROKE

This condition is commonly referred to erroneously as 'the sweats' (ferrets are actually incapable of sweating because they have no sweat glands). It is most commonly caused by the position of the cage, not allowing or creating enough shade. Alternatively, it can be caused when out working, when the carrying box is left in direct sunlight or even in a locked vehicle, where temperatures can rise dramatically.

Clinical presentation is usually agitation and distress. If they are in their cage, the ferrets will often stretch out in an attempt to cool themselves, and pant heavily. If no action is taken, or action is not taken promptly enough, they will pass out, become comatose, and will eventually die.

At the first suspicion of heatstroke, act immediately. The animal is overheating, so you must cool down both it and its environment. In extremely mild cases you may simply be able to move the cage to a more suitable position (which you should do anyway). Usually the situation is more severe, unless you are very lucky, and you will have to take more drastic measures. The best way of cooling the ferret, without shocking it, is to spray it with cool water. Also encourage it to drink cool water, from a dish if necessary. If after these emergency steps have been taken you have any further concerns, consult a vet.

HYPOCALCAEMIA

This is a lack of calcium in the blood, usually caused by the feeding of an inadequate diet. It is usually discovered whilst investigating the cause of conditions such as posterior paralysis (*see* page 93) through routine blood analysis.

Treatment is commonly via injections and feeding a calcium-rich diet.

INFLUENZA

A number of strains of the human influenza virus can infect ferrets. Transmission of the disease from humans to ferrets, ferrets to humans, and ferret to ferret is easily accomplished in aerosol droplets carried on the breath.

Clinical presentations are coughing, sneezing, runny eyes and nose, lethargy, sometimes photophobia and conjunctivitis. Very young kits may develop a much more severe upper respiratory infection, leading to death after a lower airway obstruction.

A veterinary surgeon should be consulted with reference to treatment. It is good to offer favourite foods to keep strength up and to actively encourage plenty of drinking to prevent dehydration.

LICE

This is another parasite that is sometimes, though not often, found on ferrets. It is an external pest, and working ferrets will almost certainly come into contact with them at some point.

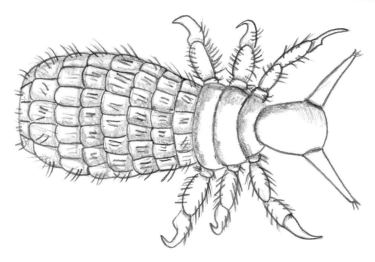

A louse, another parasite sometimes found on ferrets.

Clinical presentation is similar to fleas, in that the ferret will be scratching excessively, and there may be blood spots in the coat as a result of this.

It is easily dealt with by the application of a good-quality pesticide spray, such as Frontline. As with fleas and ticks, all bedding must be burned and replaced, and the cage or court treated.

Note: again, as with ticks and fleas, pregnant or nursing jills should not be treated due to the risk of harming or killing the kits.

MASTITIS

This is an inflammation of the jill's mammary glands. It usually occurs shortly after the birth of a litter, or after the third week of lactation, when the litter tend to demand large quantities of milk, which stresses the mother. In addition to this, the kits have teeth that can damage the nipples. It is a very painful condition that requires immediate medical attention.

Clinical presentations are firm nipples, usually red or purple in colour, which are hard and painful to the jill. The kits will probably be able to obtain little or even no milk. In acute cases the glands may become gangrenous in as little as a few hours after first being noticed. In this case the tissue turns black, and the jill will become extremely ill and dehydrated.

The ferret must be treated by a vet immediately, with broad-spectrum antibiotics. In the case of gangrenous nipples, the necrotic tissue will have to be surgically removed. After handling the ill ferret, handlers *must* wash hands thoroughly before handling others, to prevent the spread of infection.

OESTROGEN-INDUCED ANAEMIA

When a jill is in oestrus (in season) the levels of oestrogen in her body rise significantly, and if she is not brought out of season her health will be seriously detrimentally affected. She will become anaemic, due to the depression of her bone marrow, and in severe cases this can result in a condition called pancytopoenia (*see* below).

Clinical presentations are anaemia (characterized by pale lips and gums), loss of weight, anorexia, alopecia, respiratory problems, darkening of faeces, and sores.

Feeding her on raw red meat may be beneficial in mild cases. In more serious cases blood transfusions will be required and may still not be effective. Prevention is better than cure and this situation can be easily avoided. To get her out of oestrus there are three options: she can be mated with a hob, she can be served by a hoblet (vasectomized hob), or she can be taken to a vet for a jill jab (an injection of hormones to bring her out of oestrus). The alternative to these, which is obviously only possible if you never want to breed from her, is to have her spayed.

PANCYTOPOENIA

This condition is the abnormal depression of all three elements of the ferret's blood. Usually it develops as a result of oestrogen-induced anaemia (*see* above). It is seriously debilitating and potentially if not usually fatal.

Clinical presentation is as for oestrogen-induced anaemia: muscular wasting, loss of weight, anorexia, alopecia, paleness of lips and gums, and respiratory difficulties.

Blood tests will need to be made for confirmation. Blood transfusions may be beneficial, however treatment is not likely to be effective. Euthanasia is probably the kindest route.

POSTERIOR PARALYSIS

This condition is also often referred to as 'the staggers'. There are multiple possible causes of paralysis in ferrets, which may be neurological, physical or dietary. Some potential causes include Aleutian disease, hypocalcaemia, spinal carcinoma, viral myelitis, vertebral trauma precipitated by injury, or an inadequate diet.

Clinical presentations are muscular wasting in the hindquarters, weakness, inability to move in a normal manner, lethargy, loss of sensation in extremities, loss of voluntary movement.

Veterinary advice should be sought immediately.

PYOMETRA

This is a condition where pus accumulates within the uterus of a jill. It can occur after the start of a pseudo pregnancy (phantom pregnancy, the result of being served by a hoblet), or on occasion when a jill is left in oestrus for too long.

Clinical presentations are typically anorexia, lethargy, dehydration and fever. The vulva will be swollen and there may also be a discharge.

Medical attention must be sought urgently. In some cases the patient will respond well to a course of antibiotics. It is also very important to ensure that she drinks plenty of water to prevent or combat dehydration. In more serious cases, an ovariohysterectomy will have to be performed, sometimes immediately, to prevent the uterus from rupturing, which would precipitate peritonitis.

RENAL FAILURE

This is the dysfunction, or failure to operate, of the ferret's kidneys. The condition can be, in some cases, a transitory event and in such instances the animal will recover. However, it is more commonly terminal.

Clinical presentation is a loss in general condition, severe weight loss, reduction in, or loss of appetite for food, increased drinking, and foul-smelling breath. On palpation the kidneys can feel hard.

Medical attention should be sought. The foul breath and appetite problems alone could, for example, be caused by a relatively simple oral problem such as gingivitis (*see* page 89). If renal failure is suspected, blood tests can be performed for the purposes of confirma-

Ticks bite through the skin of the animal and suck its blood.

tion. If it is diagnosed, euthanasia is recommended as there is no cure and the animal would otherwise waste away and die slowly, without dignity.

TICKS

These are parasites that infest the ferret, biting through the skin and sucking blood from the host animal.

Clinical presentation is obvious – an external parasite attached to the ferret's body.

Some recommend burning the tick with a lighted cigarette, but it is far too easy to burn the ferret instead. There are various tools on the market for the removal of such pests; whichever method is employed, it is important to remove *all* of the tick. It is easy to leave the mouth parts behind and this may result in an abscess. It is said that if you grasp the tick between your finger and thumb, and rotate it one and a half times, it will let go. Alternatively, use a pair of thin, curved tweezers to grasp the tick by its mouth parts and remove it. Again, prevention is better than cure and it is wise to treat the ferrets' coats periodically with Frontline. As with all parasitic infestations, all bedding and litter must be removed and burned and the domicile treated prior to installing fresh litter and bedding.

Note: pregnant or nursing jills should not be treated due to the risk of harming or killing the young.

TRICOBEZOARS

These are balls of hair that accumulate within the intestines of the affected animal. The most common time for this occurrence is during a period of moulting. They can cause the normal passage of food to be inhibited, resulting in illness and possibly death.

Clinical presentations are loss of appetite, lethargy, listlessness, visible pain and discomfort, vomiting and weight loss. Sometimes experienced or trained hands may be able to identify the mass by gentle palpation.

Veterinary attention must be sought. Sometimes it is possible to induce small masses to be passed naturally with the employment of gastric lubricants, such as cat laxatives. More severe cases will warrant further investigation, usually by X-ray initially, followed by surgical removal. Recovery is commonly swift, and the prognosis is good.

ZINC TOXICITY

This is a condition that should be relatively easy to prevent. Ferrets are unable to endure increased, or high levels of zinc in their system. Primary sources of this metal in the ferret's environment are likely to be items such as drinkers, feed dishes, or other receptacles that are made of metal that has been galvanized to make them longer-lasting. Such items are better manufactured from stainless steel, as this also eliminates them as a source of zinc. Cage wires are typically made of galvanized twill weld or weld mesh and the ferrets may ingest the zinc by licking or chewing at the treated surfaces.

Clinical presentations are hindquarters' weakness, lethargy and anaemia. Renal failure usually follows.

As in all cases of illness, a vet must be consulted for tests and diagnosis. If this condition is confirmed, there is no cure or treatment, and euthanasia will probably be recommended in the interests of kindness.

Index

Abscesses 83
Actinomycosis 23, 83
Albino 20
Aleutian disease 83
Alopecia 84

Badger 60
Barking 60
Bites & stings 84
Blind stop 68
Bolt holes 64
Botulism 84
Breeders 16
Breeding fettle 28, 29
Breeding records 28
Broken teeth 85

Cages 12
Camouflage 44
Cancer 85
Canine distemper 86
Canine teeth 34
Canker 86
Carnivores 21
Carrying box 47, 48
Castrated 19
Cataracts 86
Chad 45
Clothing 43
Copulation 30
Coupling 30, 31
Courts 13
Cubs 12

Day old chicks 22
Deciduous teeth 34
Dehydration 23, 26, 92
Despatch 41, 55
Dressing 72
Drinking 14, 25
Droppings 63
Dry food 23
Ear mites 87
Egg yolk 32

Ferret finder 50
Fibre 21
Field craft 40

Fleas 21, 88
Foot rot 26

Gastro intestinal foreign bod-
    ies 89
Gender 18
Gestation 31
Gingivitis 89
Graft 45
Guard hairs 31

Heatstroke 13, 89
Hob 18
Hobble 19
Hoblet 19, 28
Hocking & legging 47, 55
Hypocalcaemia 22, 90

Influenza 90

Jill 7, 18
Jill jab 19, 28

Kit 17
Kittens 32

Lice 90
Lie up 68
Life span 16
Lights 23
Lime scale 25
Liver 21, 23
Liver fluke 74
Locator collars 40
Long & gate nets 51

Mammary glands 33
Marking 68
Mastitis 33, 91
Mate 18, 19
Mating 29-31
Milk sops 21
Muzzling 39

Nest 31, 32
Nettles 60
Neutered 19
Norfolk long graft 46

Nursing 32

Oesophagus 23
Oestrogen induced anaemia
    18, 92
Oestrus 19, 28
Osteodystrophy 22
Ovulation 30

Pancytopoenia 18, 92
Paunching 47, 70
Peeing 69, 70
Phantom pregnancy 18, 19
Phenol 39
Photoperiodic 28
Poaching 58
Poley 20
Posterior paralysis 93
Priest 55
Purse nets 44, 64
Pyometra 18, 93

Rabbit ìnestsî 70
Renal failure 93

Season 18, 29
Secateurs 52
Security 10, 15
Sexual dimorphism 18
Shavings 15
Shooting over 71
Skulky 38, 71
Staggers 93
Strangling 38
Suckle 31
Sweats 13

Testicles 28
Thiamine deficiency 22
Ticks 21, 71
Tricobezoars 95

Vasectomised 19
Vulva 28

Weaning 34

Zinc toxicity 95